2019
CHASE'S
Calendar of Events

ROWMAN & LITTLEFIELD
Lanham • Boulder • New York • London

Published by Rowman & Littlefield
A wholly owned subsidiary of The Rowman & Littlefield Publishing Group, Inc.
4501 Forbes Boulevard, Suite 200, Lanham, Maryland 20706
www.rowman.com
800-865-3457

Unit A, Whitacre Mews, 26-34 Stannary Street, London SE11 4AB

NOTICE
Events listed herein are not necessarily endorsed by the editors or publisher. Every effort has been made to assure the correctness of all entries, but neither the editors nor the publisher can warrant their accuracy. IT IS IMPERATIVE, IF FINANCIAL PLANS ARE TO BE MADE IN CONNECTION WITH THE DATES OR EVENTS LISTED HEREIN, THAT PRINCIPALS BE CONSULTED FOR FINAL INFORMATION.

About the Companion Website:
The companion website to *Chase's Calendar of Events 2019* is available only to purchasers of this edition. Please see page 752 for more details.

Note: The companion website will be available to users only from October 1, 2018, through December 31, 2019.

ISBN: 978-1-64143-263-4
E-ISBN: 978-1-64143-264-1
ISSN: 0740-5286

∞™ The paper used in this publication meets the minimum requirements of American National Standard for Information Sciences—Permanence of Paper for Printed Library Materials, ANSI/NISO Z39.48-1992.

Printed in the United States of America

◆ **Contents** ◆

◆ Introduction ◆

We are pleased to welcome you to *Chase's Calendar of Events 2019*, the 62nd edition of this publication. *Chase's* was first published by brothers William D. and Harrison Chase on Dec 4, 1957, as a 32-page pamphlet with 364 entries, meant to be, as Bill Chase has said, "A reliable guide to known events of the forthcoming year [1958]." That first edition was enthusiastically embraced by libraries, teachers, newspapers, broadcasters and planners in almost every conceivable branch of human activity from hospitals and nursing homes to charitable organizations to federal government agencies and officials. Not to mention the general public.

In 1958, the US Chamber of Commerce invited the Chases to incorporate their publication, *Special Days, Weeks and Months*, which listed commercial promotions. The content grew and matured to have an international scope. In 1987, celebrity birthdays were added—a popular feature. Through the years, the extended Chase's clan had helped prepare each edition, among them Helen Chase, wife of William, and their children. Harrison retired from the book in 1969, and the rest of the Chases retired in 1987—but have remained consultants and a treasured resource to the current *Chase's* staff based in Chicago, IL.

Today, *Chase's* is a combination book/searchable website with 12,500 entries in a range of subject areas—plus exhaustive appendices. All entries are updated and thoroughly fact-checked, making *Chase's* the most respected and comprehensive reference available on holidays, special events, international days of celebration, federal and state observances, historic and birth anniversaries and special days, weeks and months. *Chase's* strives to deliver interesting facts every day of the year.

What's New in 2019

2019 is the International Year of the Periodic Table of Chemical Elements, the International Year of Indigenous Languages and the International Year of Moderation. This year sees a rare Transit of Mercury as well as a total solar eclipse. Major sporting events include the Pan American Games, FIFA Women's World Cup, Special Olympics World Summer Games, Cricket World Cup and Rugby World Cup, among others.

2019 ushers in a great variety of key birth anniversaries: the 500th death anniversary of artist and inventor Leonardo da Vinci, the 200th birth anniversaries of Queen Victoria and poet Walt Whitman, the 150th birth anniversary of Mahatma Gandhi, the 100th birth anniversary of Jackie Robinson and more. Historical anniversaries of note include the 75th anniversary of D-Day and the 50th anniversary of the moon landing. The famed concert at Woodstock and the Stonewall Riots also took place in 1969. All of these and more are discussed more fully in the "Spotlight" section.

New special days, weeks and months can be found throughout the main calendar section, so look out for observances such as National Quinoa Day (Jan 16), National Backcountry Ski Day (Mar 4), World Bicycle Day (June 3), Living Dead Day (Oct 1), National Sports Fan Day (Nov 1), National Pollinator Week (June 17–23) and much more.

Types of Entries in *Chase's Calendar of Events*

Astronomical Phenomena

Information about eclipses, equinoxes and solstices, moon phases and other astronomical phenomena is calculated from data prepared by the US Naval Observatory and Her Majesty's Nautical Almanac Office. **Please note: in *Chase's*, Universal Time has been converted to Eastern Time.**

Religious Observances

Principal observances of the Christian, Jewish, Muslim and Baha'i faiths are presented with background information from their respective calendars. We include anticipated dates for Muslim holidays. When known, religious events of China, Japan and India are also listed. There is no single Hindu calendar and different sects define the Hindu lunar month differently. There is no single lunar calendar that serves as a model for all Buddhists, either. Therefore, we are not able to provide the dates of many religious holidays for these faiths.

National and International Observances and Civic Holidays

Chase's features independence days, national days and public holidays from around the world. Technically, there are no national holidays in the US: holidays proclaimed by the president only apply to federal employees and to the District of Columbia. State governors proclaim holidays for their states. In practice, federal holidays are usually proclaimed by governors as well. Some governors proclaim commemorative days that are unique to their state.

Special Days, Weeks and Months

Whether it's Black History Month, National Police Week or National Grandparents' Day, the annual calendar has myriad special days, weeks and months. Since 1957, *Chase's* has been the most comprehensive and authoritative reference of these. Until January 1995, Congress had been active in seeing that special observances were commemorated. Members of the Senate and House could introduce legislation for a special observance to commemorate people, events and other activities they thought worthy of national recognition. Because these bills took up a disproportionate amount of time on the part of congressmen and their staffs, Congress decided to discontinue this process in January 1995 when it reviewed and reformed its rules and practices.

Today, Congress does from time to time issue commemorative resolutions, which do not have the force of law. The president of the US has the authority to declare any commemorative event by proclamation, but this is done infrequently. (Some state legislatures and governors proclaim special days, weeks and months, as do mayors of cities.)

So where do all these special days, weeks and months come from? The majority come from national organizations that use their observances for public outreach and to plan specific events. For special months regarding health issues, for example, you can expect to see more information disseminated, special commemorative walks and medical screenings during that month. The *Chase's* editorial staff includes a special day, week or month in the annual reference based on the authority of the organization observing it, how many years it has been observed, the amount of promotion and activities that are a part of it, its uniqueness and a variety of other factors. (We also include a list of 2019 special months in our appendix section.)

Presidential Proclamations

As we noted above, the president has the authority to declare any commemorative event by proclamation. A good number of these will be proclamations for which there has been legislation giving continuing authority for a proclamation to be issued each year. Mother's Day, for example, has been proclaimed since 1914 by public resolution. The White House Clerk's Office initiates the issuing of these proclamations each year, since they are mandated by authorizing legislation. Of course, there will be new ones: Patriot Day (in the wake of the Sept

11, 2001, terrorist attacks) is an example. In *Chase's* we list proclamations that have continuing authority and those that have been issued consistently since 2008 in the main calendar of the book. In our text, ★ indicates a presidential proclamation. In our appendix, we also offer a complete list of proclamations issued from Jan 1, 2017, to June 15, 2018.

Events and Festivals

Chase's includes national and international special events as well as festivals defined by their uniqueness and their finite brief length of time. Sporting events; book, film, food and other festivals; seasonal celebrations; folkloric events (Up Helly Aa or Carnival, for example); music outings and more make up these types of entries. These entries are usually sponsored: they have contact information for the general public and all information in the entry comes from the sponsor (see below on sponsored events).

Anniversaries

Anniversaries include historic (creation of nations or states, battles, inventions, publications of note, popular culture events, famous firsts, etc) and biographical (birth or death anniversaries of notable personages) milestones.

Birthdays Today

Living celebrities in politics, the arts, sports and popular culture are included in the "Birthdays Today" section following each calendar day. If there is a question about the birth day or year, this is noted. **Be aware that national and international political leaders (US president, US governors and senators, prime ministers, cabinet officials, etc) listed are current as of July 2018.**

Spotlight

The tinted pages starting off *Chase's Calendar of Events* form the "Spotlight" section. In a book as packed as *Chase's*, the reader may need a little help picking out significant anniversaries and events for the current year, and "Spotlight" is the answer to that need. We cover significant 2019 historical and birth anniversaries as well as major events with a little more depth than in the main calendar section.

New Style Versus Old Style Dates

Please note that dates for historic events can be assumed to be Gregorian calendar (New Style) dates unless "(OS)" appears after the date. This annotation means that the date in question is an Old Style, or Julian calendar, date. Most of America's founders were born before 1752, when Great Britain and its colonies adopted the Gregorian calendar. As an example of this, we list George Washington's birthday as Feb 22, 1732, which is the Gregorian or New Style date. However, when he was born Great Britain and its colonies began the year on Mar 25, not Jan 1, so his Julian birthdate was Feb 11, 1731.

About Sponsored Events

Events for which there is individual or organizational sponsorship are listed with the name of the event, inclusive dates of observance, a brief description, estimated attendance figures and the sponsor's name and contact information. We obtain information for these events directly from the sponsors. There is no fee to be listed in *Chase's* and sponsors submit events to be chosen at the discretion of the *Chase's* editors. Neither the editors nor the publisher necessarily endorse these events.

About the Companion Website

Purchasers of *Chase's Calendar of Events 2019* have access to an exclusive companion website from October 2018 to Dec 31, 2019. This website offers many ways to search 2019 content digitally. Please go to page 752 to get the URL (the website's address) and the password as well as more information on certain features. (Please note that www.chases.com is still the general marketing website for *Chase's Calendar of Events*—it is not the companion website.)

Acknowledgments

A book the size of *Chase's* comes about through the care and attention of many organizations and people. The editors and publisher would like to thank the event sponsors; CVBs; chambers of commerce; tourism agencies; nonprofit organizations; publicists; festival organizers; historians; museum directors; librarians; National Park Service employees; embassy and cultural affairs staffs; astronomers; national, state and local government officials and many others who help us put together this reference every year.

Bill Chase and his family continue to support and inspire the *Chase's* project! In Bill Chase there's no better advocate of holidays and celebrations—he led the way for the "democratization" of special days, weeks and months. He and his family are the proud sponsors of several special days.

We offer grateful thanks to the researchers, writers and fact-checkers who helped us to assemble the 2019 edition: Rob Walton, Loretta Ullrich-Ferguson, Madeleine Marchaterre Super, Joel Super, Johnny Loftus, Sandy Whiteley, James Foster, Gigi Grajdura and Hannah Krog.

Thank you to our editorial and production colleagues at Bernan Press and Rowman & Littlefield: Patricia Stevenson, Emily Eastridge, Karen Ackermann, Chloe Batch, Joyce Culley, Ira Sumarno, Maiyanna Ridgley, Al Hinds and Cecil Richards. Thank you also to Mary Meghan Ryan and Veronica Dove at Bernan Press; Paul Konowitch, publisher, Bernan Press; and Jed Lyons, president and CEO of Rowman & Littlefield.

HOLLY McGUIRE, *Editor in Chief*
July 2018

Spotlight on the Past

1919

100 YEARS AGO

Landmark World Events

Jan 3 Faisal-Weizmann Agreement for Arab-Jewish cooperation in the development of a Jewish homeland in Palestine and an Arab nation in a large part of the Middle East was signed.

Jan 15 Revolutionary Socialist Rosa Luxemburg was tortured and murdered by paramilitary troops in Berlin, Germany.

Jan 18 Versailles Peace Conference opened in Paris with delegates from 27 victorious nations.

Jan 25 The League of Nations was created at the Paris Peace Conference in France as the first international organization with the mission to maintain world peace. Its first meeting took place a year later. The United States never participated.

Feb 6 A new German Republic was declared at the city of Weimar. A constitution was adopted Aug 11.

Mar 23 Benito Mussolini founded his Fascist political movement in Italy.

Apr 10 Mexican revolutionary leader Emiliano Zapata was ambushed and killed at Chinameca, Mexico.

Apr 13 Jallianwalla Bagh Massacre. In Amritsar, India, the British Indian Army fired on Sikh pilgrims gathered for a religious festival in Jallianwalla Bagh, Punjab. Reports of casualties ranged from 379 to more than 1,000.

May 19 Ataturk organized resistance to the dismemberment of the Ottoman Empire following WWI, beginning the Turkish War of Independence.

June 14 First nonstop transatlantic flight left St. John's, Newfoundland, Canada, landing in Ireland on June 15. British pilots John Alcock and Arthur Whitten Brown made the crossing in 16 hours and won the 10,000 pounds offered as a prize by an English newspaper.

June 28 The Treaty of Versailles was signed at the palace of Versailles, in France, formally ending World War I. The United States never ratified this treaty.

Aug 19 Afghanistan gained independence from the United Kingdom.

Sept 3 Jan Smuts became the second prime minister of South Africa.

Dec 1 American-born Nancy, Viscountess Astor, became the first woman to take a seat in the British House of Commons.

■ The Nobel Peace Prize was awarded to American President Woodrow Wilson.

Landmark US Events

Jan 15 In the Great Molasses Flood in Boston, MA, a large wave of molasses was ejected from an exploding storage tank, killing 21.

Feb 6–11 A general strike in Seattle, WA, saw more than 60,000 union workers from 110 locals in work stoppage. This was the first general strike in the United States. Seattle's population at the time was 315,000.

Feb 15 The American Legion was organized in Paris.

Feb 26 The Grand Canyon and Lafayette National Monument (later renamed Acadia) were designated national parks. Zion National Park was founded on Nov 19.

Mar 13 A letter bearing this date and a return address of "Hell" was sent to the *Times-Picayune* from a

🔍 The Axeman of New Orleans

On Mar 13, 1919, a serial killer who had terrified New Orleans small merchants and their families with indiscriminate slaughter sent a letter to the *Times-Picayune*. Signed "The Axeman," this letter gave a promise to suspend his murders if jazz was playing on the night of March 18–19: "I am very fond of jazz music, and I swear by all the devils in the nether regions that every person shall be spared in whose home a jazz band is in full swing at the time I have just mentioned. If everyone has a jazz band going, well, then, so much the better for you people. One thing is certain and that is that some of your people who do not jazz it out on that specific Tuesday night (if there be any) will get the axe." The city went wild with clubs booking jazz groups and homeowners playing their gramophones. The serial killer kept his word for that night but resumed his murders in August. In a spree beginning in May 1918 and lasting until October 1919, the Axeman killed six people and injured twelve.

serial killer who called himself The Axeman.

April–May Followers of the Italian anarchist Luigi Galleani (the Galleanists) attempted to send package bombs to 36 prominent politicians and business people. Most of the packages were intercepted before they reached their targets. But the housekeeper and wife of US Senator Thomas W. Hardwick (Georgia) were severely injured. This was the beginning of a series of anarchist bombings—the "Red Scare" of 1919.

June 2 Galleanists set off eight bombs in eight US cities. One victim was killed and one terrorist

died when his bomb prematurely exploded.

June 4 Congress approved the 19th Amendment affirming a woman's right to vote and submitted it to the states for ratification (which came in 1920).

July 27 Chicago race riots began after a black boy was killed on a segregated beach. See "Spotlight on American Anniversaries."

Sept 2 The Communist Party of America was founded in Chicago, IL.

Sept 9 The Boston Police Strike began.

Sept 10–15 Florida Keys hurricane killed 600 in Florida and Texas.

Oct 2 US President Woodrow Wilson, weakened by vigorous campaigning for the Treaty of Versailles and the League of Nations, was cut down by a stroke that left him an invalid.

Oct 28 The 18th Amendment, passed by Congress in 1917, forbidding the manufacture and sale of alcohol, was ratified by the states this year. The Volstead Act, the enabling legislation to enforce the amendment, was passed on this date and went into effect in 1920.

Nov 11 The first Armistice Day was celebrated in the United States.

Dec 21 Political activist Emma Goldman, along with more than 200 others, was deported to the Soviet Union, a result of the "Red Scare."

■ The University of California at Los Angeles was opened as the Southern Branch of the University of California.

The "Red Scare" of 1919

Fueled by strong nationalist, anti-immigrant sentiment, the Red Scare of 1919 was the result of the fear many Americans were suffering from slowing production, rising unemployment and inflation after WWI. Labor union membership was on the rise, as were stagnating wages, job insecurity and poor working conditions, providing a perfect catalyst for civil unrest. Police, shipyard, coal and steel workers all went on strike in 1919 to advocate for job security, better wages and safer working conditions; economic insecurity and competition for employment, particularly during the strikes, exacerbated existing racial tensions, resulting in race riots in over three dozen cities, notably Chicago and Washington, DC, during the Red Summer of 1919.

Underpinning it all was a layer of intense suspicion of Communist, Socialist and anarchist sympathizers following the violent overthrow of the Russian monarchy during the Bolshevik Revolution in 1917, leading to heightened fear that Russian immigrants would overthrow the US government. Citizens' freedom of expression was limited, notably through "red flag laws" and the Sedition and Immigration Acts of 1918. The Overman Committee's investigation and report further stoked nativist sentiment with its depiction of Russians as "human scum," as did May Day rioting and anarchist bombings in April and June, which targeted, among others, US Attorney General A. Mitchell Palmer and Supreme Court Justice Oliver Wendell Holmes, Jr. In response, Palmer conducted his eponymous raids, during which federal agents captured, arrested and deported many immigrants, particularly those of Eastern European descent. Although fears abated in 1920, the period was influential in the formation of laws enacted in 1921 limiting immigration, which were made permanent in the Immigration Act of 1924.

Culture

Literary Arts

■ The Nobel Prize for Literature was awarded to Swiss poet Carl Friedrich Georg Spitteler.

■ The Algonquin Round Table, a group of writers, actors and wits led by Alexander Woollcott, first met at the Algonquin Hotel in New York.

Fiction

- *The Moon and Sixpence*, by W. Somerset Maugham
- *Winesburg, Ohio*, short stories by Sherwood Anderson
- *My Man Jeeves*, by P.G. Wodehouse
- *Night and Day*, by Virginia Woolf
- *The Haunted Bookshop*, by Christopher Morley
- "In the Penal Colony," by Franz Kafka published in Germany

Nonfiction

- *The American Language*, by H.L. Mencken
- *Ten Days that Shook the World*, by John Reed
- *Introduction to Mathematical Philosophy*, by Bertrand Russell
- *The Economic Consequences of the Peace*, by John Maynard Keynes
- *The Elements of Style*, by William Strunk, Jr

Poetry

- *War Poems*, by Siegfried Sassoon
- *The Wild Swans at Coole*, by William Butler Yeats, was first published in the United States this year.
- *Modern American Poetry*, anthology edited by Louis Untermeyer

Children's Literature

- *Lad: A Dog*, by Albert Payson Terhune
- *Jungle Tales of Tarzan*, by Edgar Rice Burroughs

Journalism

- *The New York Daily News* began publication and became the most widely read paper in the United States.

- "Gasoline Alley," a newspaper comic strip by Frank King, began national syndication this year.

Theater and Opera

- *Clarence*, by Booth Tarkington, starring Alfred Lunt
- *Mr. Pim Passes By*, by A.A. Milne
- *Die Frau ohne Schatten*, opera by Richard Strauss, produced in Vienna
- *Apple Blossoms*, musical with Fred Astaire and his sister Adele
- *La, La, Lucille*, with music by George Gershwin
- *Angel Face*, with music by Victor Herbert and H.B. Smith
- *The Ziegfeld Follies of 1919*, with music by Irving Berlin and others, starring Eddie Cantor

Film

Nov 9 Felix the Cat made his first cartoon appearance in "Feline Follies."

- *The Miracle Man*, starring Lon Chaney
- *Daddy-Long-Legs*, starring Mary Pickford
- *Broken Blossoms*, directed by D.W. Griffith, starring Lillian Gish
- *Till the Clouds Roll By*, starring Douglas Fairbanks
- *Male and Female*, directed by Cecil B. DeMille, starring Gloria Swanson
- *Madame DuBarry* (released in the United States as *Passion*), directed by Ernst Lubitsch and starring Pola Negri and Emil Jannings

Radio

- Lee De Forest resumed broadcasting from the Bronx after a hiatus caused by WWI.

- The Marconi Company launched an experimental station in Montreal, QC, Canada.

Music

- *The Three-Cornered Hat*, by Manuel de Falla, had its world premiere in London, England.
- *Concerto for Violincello and Orchestra*, by Edward Elgar, premiered in London.
- *Mirages*, by Gabriel Faure, premiered in Paris, France.
- The Los Angeles Philharmonic Orchestra was founded.

Popular Songs

- Irving Berlin, "A Pretty Girl Is Like a Melody"
- Clarence Williams and C. Warfield, "Baby, Won't You Please Come Home"
- Jelly Roll Morton, "Kansas City Stomp"
- Charles L. Johnson, "Sweet and Low"
- John Philip Sousa, "The Golden Star March"
- Victor Herbert, "Indian Summer: An American Idyll"

Art

- Walter Gropius, an architect, founded the Bauhaus movement in Weimar, Germany. See "Spotlight on World Anniversaries."
- *The Murder*, by Edvard Munch
- *Falling Bird*, by Paul Klee

- *Bird in Space*, sculpture by Constantine Brancusi
- *Fifth Avenue*, by Childe Hassam
- *Blue Line*, by Georgia O'Keeffe

Science and Technology

- The Nobel Prize for Physics was awarded to German scientist Johannes Stark for his work on the Doppler effect in canal rays and the splitting of spectral lines in electric fields.
- The Nobel Prize for Medicine or Physiology was awarded to Belgian scientist Jules Bordet for his discoveries related to immunity.
- The Nobel Prize for Chemistry was not awarded this year.
- Neon was the first element to be analyzed by mass spectrometer by English physicist Francis William Aston.
- Scientific proof of Einstein's Theory of Relativity was obtained during a total eclipse of the sun by British astronomer Arthur Stanley Eddington.
- Rickets were found by Edward Mellanby not to be an infectious disease but a vitamin deficiency.

Commerce and New Products

Jan 18 Bentley Motors Limited was founded by W.O. Bentley in London, England. The first car was produced that same year.

Oct 7 Dutch airline KLM was established.

- The French fragrance house of Caron introduced Tabac Blonde, a perfume specifically designed for women who smoked—reflecting the postwar break from traditional norms by women.
- Sunkist oranges were the first fruit to be trademarked.
- Hilton Hotel Corp. was founded in Cisco, TX, by Conrad Hilton.
- The Radio Corporation of America (RCA) was founded.
- The Frigidaire brand was produced by General Motors.

Sports

- The flu pandemic of 1918–19 and the aftermath of WWI curtailed many sporting events.

Auto Racing

- The Indianapolis 500 was won by Howdy Wilcox driving a Peugeot at 100 miles per hour.

Baseball

Oct 1–9 World Series took place with the Cincinnati Reds defeating the Chicago White Sox. But it was quickly revealed that some White Sox players conspired to lose the series in what became known as the Black Sox Scandal. See "Spotlight on American Anniversaries."

- Babe Ruth hit 29 home runs for the Boston Red Sox, breaking the single season record.

Basketball

- Minnesota was the leading college team, with a record of 13–0.
- Professional teams were often "barnstormers" that traveled around the country playing local teams for money. Several regional leagues in the northeast resumed after the war or began competition this year.

Boxing

- Jack Dempsey won the World Heavyweight Boxing Championship.

Football

- There was no clear champion in NCAA football. Notre Dame, Centre College, Harvard, Illinois and Texas A&M were all named champions by different selectors.
- Illinois was the Big Ten champion.
- As in the previous year, the Rose Bowl was contested by military teams instead of college teams. The Great Lakes Navy team defeated the Mare Island Marines.
- The Green Bay Packers were founded as a professional football team by coach Curly Lambeau.

Golf

- Walter Hagen won the US Open.
- Jim Barnes won the USPGA championship.

Hockey

- The Stanley Cup finals were canceled after a player contracted the Spanish flu.

Horse Racing

- Sir Barton, ridden by Johnny Loftus, became the first horse to win the Triple Crown: the Kentucky Derby, the Preakness Stakes and the Belmont Stakes.

Tennis

- Bill Johnston won the men's singles at the US Open.
- Hazel Hotchkiss Wightman won the women's singles at the US Open.
- Australian Gerald Patterson won the men's singles at Wimbledon.

- Frenchwoman Suzanne Lenglen won the women's singles at Wimbledon.

1919 Deaths

- L. Frank Baum, author of *The Wizard of Oz*
- Louis Botha, first prime minister of South Africa
- Andrew Carnegie, steel magnate and philanthropist
- Raymonde de Laroche, first woman to receive a pilot's license
- Jane Delano, pioneering and influential American nurse
- Hermann Emil Fischer, German chemist and Nobel Prize recipient
- Henry Clay Frick, coal baron and art collector
- Karl Adolph Gjellerup, Danish poet and author, Nobel Prize recipient
- Gojong, first emperor of Korea
- Ernst Haeckel, German zoologist who named thousands of species
- Oscar Hammerstein I, German opera impresario
- Prince John, youngest child of England's King George V
- Augustus Juilliard, millionaire whose estate founded the Juilliard School of Music
- Wilfred Laurier, seventh prime minister of Canada
- Jean Navarre, highly decorated French WWI ace
- Pierre-Auguste Renoir, French painter
- Theodore Roosevelt, 26th US president

- Alfred Werner, Swiss chemist and Nobel Prize recipient
- F.W. Woolworth, dime store magnate
- Emiliano Zapata, Mexican revolutionary leader

1944

75 YEARS AGO

Landmark World Events

Jan 12 British Prime Minister Winston Churchill and Leader of Free France Charles de Gaulle met to discuss war aims in Marrakech, Morocco.

Jan 27 The siege of Leningrad was lifted. See "Spotlight on World Anniversaries."

Mar 25 In the "Great Escape," 76 Royal Air Force captives escaped from a German POW camp through a tunnel. Seventy-three of them were recaptured, and fifty were executed. Only three made it to safety.

June 4 Allied troops entered Rome.

June 6 On D-Day, Operation Overlord commenced, with Allied troops landing in northern France. See "Spotlight on World Anniversaries."

June 13 The first of more than 8,000 V-1 cruise missiles was launched by Germany at British civilian targets.

June 17 Iceland declared its independence from Denmark.

June 19 The Battle of the Philippine Sea ended with the loss of 402 Japanese planes and only 27 US

planes. It was the greatest carrier battle of WWII.

July 10 Tokyo was bombed for the first time since the Doolittle raid in 1942.

July 20 German army officer Claus von Stauffenberg and others attempted the assassination of Adolf Hitler by a briefcase bomb at Hitler's "Wolf's Lair" military headquarters in East Prussia. Hitler survived the blast. On July 21, von Stauffenberg was shot, and many of the plotters were hung or shot on Aug 8 and 9.

July 24 Majdanek in Poland was the first concentration camp to be liberated by Allied (Soviet) troops.

Aug 1 In the Warsaw Uprising, the Polish Home Army revolted against German occupiers, assuming the nearby Red Army would come to their aid. By Oct 2, the German army had put down the uprising, the Soviets never having given help to the Poles.

Aug 10 At the conclusion of the Second Battle of Guam (commenced July 21), Guam fell to Allied troops. All of the Mariana Islands were now in Allied hands.

Aug 15 Allied forces landed in southern France and advanced rapidly northeast. The German army retreated toward Germany.

Aug 21–Oct 7 Representatives from China, Great Britain, the Soviet Union and the United States met at Dunbarton Oaks, an estate in Washington, DC, to set up the basic structure of the United Nations.

Aug 24–25 French and US forces liberated Paris. General de Gaulle led French troops down the Champs-Elysees the next day.

Sept 3 Anne Frank and her family were deported on the last train to Auschwitz. On Oct 30, she was transferred to Bergen-Belsen, where she died in early 1945 at age 15.

Sept 9 The first V-2 rocket landed in London, England. More than 3,000 of these long-range guided ballistic missiles hit London and cities in Belgium. They were the first man-made objects to reach the edge of space.

Sept 12 At the Second Quebec Conference, Churchill and US President Franklin D. Roosevelt discussed military cooperation in the Pacific and the future of Germany.

Sept 13 American troops reached the Siegfried Line, the western edge of Germany's defenses.

October 9 At the Moscow Conference, Soviet Premier Joseph Stalin and Churchill discussed spheres of influence in the postwar Balkans.

Oct 20 In the Battle of Leyte Gulf, the Philippines were invaded by US troops and General Douglas MacArthur fulfilled his promise, "I shall return."

Nov 20 German Führer Adolf Hitler moved to his bunker in Berlin.

Dec 16 In the Battle of the Bulge, a surprise German offensive in the Ardennes forest, German lines advanced, creating a bulge into Allied territory. By Jan 25, 1945, the Allies had regained their original territory.

■ The Nobel Peace Prize was awarded to the International Committee of the Red Cross.

Landmark US Events

Jan 29 The USS *Missouri* launched at Brooklyn Navy Yard. It would be used as the site for the signing of the peace treaty with Japan in 1945.

Feb 4 The Bronze Star was established as an award for members of the Armed Forces for valor in combat. Civilians are also eligible for the medal.

Apr 3 The Supreme Court ruled in *Smith v. Allwright* that Americans cannot be denied the right to vote because of their color.

June 12 President Roosevelt gave his last Fireside Chat, on Opening the Fifth War Loan Drive.

June 22 Congress enacted the GI Bill of Rights, giving veterans education and housing benefits.

July 6 In Hartford, CT, the main tent of the Ringling Bros. and Barnum & Bailey Circus caught fire, killing more than 160 people, many of them children.

Oct 20 A liquefied natural gas explosion leveled one square mile of Cleveland, OH, killing 130 people.

Nov 7 Franklin Delano Roosevelt won an unprecedented fourth term as US president, defeating Thomas E. Dewey, but he lived to serve only 11 weeks of his term.

Dec 14 The five-star grade for generals of the army was established. First awarded to generals Eisenhower, MacArthur, Marshall and Arnold.

■ The United Negro College Fund was established by Frederick Patterson and Mary McLeod Bethune.

■ The US Forest Service and the Ad Council released the first posters to feature Smokey Bear.

Culture

Literary Arts

■ The Nobel Prize for Literature was won by Danish novelist Johannes Vilhelm Jensen.

Fiction

■ *The Dangling Man*, by Saul Bellow

■ *A Bell for Adano*, by John Hersey

■ *The Lost Weekend*, by Charles R. Jackson

■ *The Horse's Mouth*, by Joyce Cary

■ *Forever Amber*, by Kathleen Winsor

Nonfiction

■ *An American Dilemma*, by Gunnar Myrdal

■ *The Road to Serfdom*, by Friedrich Hayek

■ *Anna and the King of Siam*, by Margaret Landon

Poetry

■ *V-Letter and Other Poems*, by Karl Shapiro

■ *1 x 1*, by E.E. Cummings

■ *For the Time Being*, W.H. Auden

■ *Land of Unlikeness*, by Robert Lowell

Children's Literature

■ *Yonie Wondernose*, by Marguerite de Angeli

■ *The Island of Adventure*, by Enid Blyton

■ *Pretzel*, by Margaret Rey and H.A. Rey

Journalism

Dec 19 The first issue of *Le Monde* was published in France.

■ Ernie Pyle won a Pulitzer Prize for his work as a war correspondent.

Theater and Opera

■ *No Exit*, a play by Jean-Paul Sartre, was published.

■ *Antigone*, by Jean Anouilh, premiered in Nazi-occupied Paris.

■ *Richard III*, starring Laurence Olivier, at the Old Vic in London.

■ *I Remember Mama*, by John Van Druten, opened in New York City.

■ *The Glass Menagerie*, by Tennessee Williams, premiered in Chicago, IL.

■ *On the Town*, with music by Leonard Bernstein, Betty Comden and Adolph Green, debuted on Broadway.

■ *Fancy Free*, a ballet choreographed by Jerome Robbins with a score by Leonard Bernstein, opened at the old Metropolitan Opera House in New York City.

■ *Song of Norway*, with music based on the compositions of Edward Grieg, opened in Los Angeles, CA.

Film

Academy Awards
(Awarded in 1945)

■ Best Picture: Going My Way

■ Best Actor: Bing Crosby, *Going My Way*

■ Best Actress: Ingrid Bergman, *Gaslight*

■ Best Director: Leo McCarey, *Going My Way*, which also won best screenplay and best song ("Would You Like to Swing on a Star," by James Van Heusen and Johnny Burke).

Notable Films

■ *Henry V*, directed and produced by Laurence Olivier, who also performed the lead role, was the first Shakespeare film in color.

■ *Meet Me in St. Louis*, starring Judy Garland and Margaret O'Brien

■ *National Velvet*, starring Elizabeth Taylor

■ *Hollywood Canteen*, with many stars playing themselves in cameo roles

■ *Thirty Seconds over Tokyo*, with Van Johnson and Spencer Tracy

Television

Sept 28 "The Boys from Boise," a full-length musical written for TV, aired on WABD in New York.

■ "Missus Goes a Shopping," one of the first game shows, on CBS

Radio

Dec 10 Arturo Toscanini conducted a performance of Beethoven's *Fidelio* on NBC radio as a statement against tyranny.

■ "The Adventures of Ozzie and Harriet," later to be a TV show

■ "Boston Blackie" on NBC

■ "The Frank Sinatra Show" on CBS

Music

Dec 15 The plane carrying big band leader and song writer Glenn Miller disappeared over the English Channel. He was awarded the Bronze Star posthumously.

■ *Piano Sonata, No. 8*, by Sergei Prokofiev, the third of his Three War Sonatas, premiered in Moscow, USSR.

■ *String Quartet No. 2 in A major*, by Dmitri Shostakovich, premiered in Leningrad, USSR.

■ *Appalachian Spring*, by Aaron Copland, debuted at the Library of Congress. The music was commissioned by Martha Graham for her ballet.

■ "Hymn of the Bolshevik Party," by Alexander Alexandrov, became the national anthem of the Soviet Union, replacing the "Internationale," which was now reserved for Communist Party functions.

■ Woody Guthrie first recorded "This Land Is Your Land."

Popular Songs

■ Cole Porter, "Don't Fence Me In"

■ Karl Suessdorf, "Moonlight in Vermont"

■ Johnny Mercer and Harold Arlen, "Ac-cent-tchu-ate the Positive"

■ Jule Styne and Sammy Cahn, "I'll Walk Alone" and "Saturday Night (Is the Loneliest Night of the Week)"

Art

- *Girl in a White Dress, Red Background* and *Annelies, White Tulips and Anemones*, by Henri Matisse

- *Rue Saint Rustique, Montmartre*, by Maurice Utrillo

- *Plantation Road*, by Thomas Hart Benton

- *The Red Stairway*, by Ben Shahn

- *Victory*, sculpture by William Zorach

Science and Technology

- The Nobel Prize for Chemistry was won by German Otto Hahn for his discovery of the fusion of heavy nuclei.

- The Nobel Prize for Physics was won by American Isidor Isaac Rabi, who recorded the magnetic properties of atomic nuclei.

- The Nobel Prize for Medicine or Physiology was won by Americans Joseph Erlanger and Herbert Spencer Gasser for their discoveries related to the highly differential functions of single nerve fibers.

- Evidence that DNA is the building block of life was discovered by Oswald Avery at the Rockefeller Institute in New York.

- Austrian pediatrician Hans Asperger published his paper "Autistic Psychopaths in Childhood," which described autism symptoms.

- The element Americium was discovered by Glenn Seaborg as part of the Manhattan Project.

- The US nuclear facility Hanford Site (established in 1943) near Hanford, WA, produced its first plutonium.

- The Mark I calculator was built at Harvard University with a grant from IBM.

Commerce and New Products

July 1–22 At the Bretton Woods Conference in New Hampshire, representatives from all 44 Allied nations met to make plans to regulate international monetary affairs and the financial order after the war. They established the International Monetary Fund and the International Bank for Reconstruction and Development (now the World Bank).

- Chiquita Banana was introduced as a brand-name product by United Fruit.

- Alaska Airlines commenced operations.

- Orbit gum was launched by Wrigley.

Sports

- The 1944 Summer and Winter Olympics were canceled.

Auto Racing

- The Indianapolis 500 was not run because of the war.

Baseball

June 6 All games were canceled due to D-Day.

Oct 4–9 The St. Louis Cardinals defeated the St. Louis Browns in the World Series, four games to two—the last World Series played entirely in one stadium (the teams shared a park). Nicknamed the "Trolley Series."

- St. Louis Browns announced they were dropping their policy restricting black fans to the bleachers.

Basketball

- Utah defeated Dartmouth for the NCAA Division I championship.

- Professional champions were the Wilmington Bombers of the American Basketball League and the Fort Wayne Zollner Pistons of the National Basketball League.

Football

- The Green Bay Packers defeated the New York Giants for the NFL championship.

- NCAA college champion: Army

- Big Ten champion: Ohio State

- The Heisman Trophy was won by Les Horvath of Ohio State.

- In the Rose Bowl, the University of Southern California defeated the University of Washington.

Golf

- The US Open was not held this year.

- Bob Hamilton was PGA champion

Hockey

Apr 4–13 The Montreal Canadiens defeated the Chicago Black Hawks for the Stanley Cup in a four-game sweep.

Horse Racing

- Pensive, ridden by Conn McCreary, won the Kentucky Derby and Preakness Stakes.

- Bounding Home, ridden by Gayle Smith, won the Belmont Stakes.

Soccer

- Philadelphia Americans were champions of the American Soccer League.

Tennis

- Frank Parker won the men's singles at the US Open.
- Pauline Betz won the women's singles at the US Open.
- Matches were not held at Wimbledon because of the war.

1944 Deaths

- Princess Beatrice, last child of Queen Victoria and Prince Albert
- Antoine de Saint-Exupery, pilot and author of *The Little Prince*
- George Herriman, American cartoonist, creator of "Krazy Kat"
- Lou Hoover, former first lady of the United States
- Florence Foster Jenkins, American socialite and famously horrible singer
- Wassily Kandinsky, Russian artist
- Joe Kennedy, Jr, oldest son in the Joseph Kennedy family
- Kenesaw Mountain Landis, commissioner of baseball
- Edwin Lutyens, architect
- Aristide Maillol, French sculptor
- Carl Mayer, screenwriter for *The Cabinet of Dr. Caligari* and *Sunrise*
- Glenn Miller, big band leader
- Piet Mondrian, Dutch artist
- Edvard Munch, Norwegian artist
- Romain Rolland, French writer and Nobel Laureate
- Erwin Rommel, German army officer, the "Desert Fox"
- Al Smith, Democratic candidate for president in 1928
- Ida Tarbell, muckraking journalist
- Lupe Velez, Mexican actress
- Wendell Willkie, Republican candidate for president in 1940
- William Allen White, newspaper editor and writer

1969

50 YEARS AGO

Landmark World Events

Jan 22 In Moscow, USSR, a disgruntled Soviet Army deserter, Viktor Ilyin, attempted to assassinate Soviet leader Leonid Brezhnev during a motorcade honoring the cosmonauts of *Soyuz* 4 and *Soyuz* 5. Some of the cosmonauts were injured.

Jan 30 In London, England, The Beatles gave their last public performance on the roof of Apple Records.

Feb 4 In Cairo, Egypt, at the meeting of the Palestinian National Council, Yasser Arafat was elected chairman of the Palestine Liberation Organization.

Mar 17 Golda Meir was elected prime minister of Israel. Meir was the first woman (and to date only woman) to hold that office.

Apr 28 Charles de Gaulle stepped down as president of France after ten years in office.

June 20 Georges Pompidou was elected president of France.

July 22 In Spain, dictator and head of state Francisco Franco appointed Prince Juan Carlos as his successor.

July 31 Pope Paul VI arrived at Entebbe, Uganda, marking the first visit of a pontiff to the African continent.

Sept 1 In Libya, a bloodless coup d'état by the military ousted King Idris and ushered Muammar Gaddafi into power—as "Brother Leader and Guide of the Revolution."

Oct 21 Six days after the assassination of President Abdirashid Ali Shermarke, General Siad Barre came to power in Somalia.

Oct 22 Willy Brandt became chancellor of the Federal Republic of Germany (West Germany).

Nov 15 Illuminating the high stakes of the ongoing Cold War, Soviet submarine *K-19* collided with the American sub USS *Gato* in the frigid waters of the Barents Sea.

Nov 17 At Helsinki, Finland, US and Soviet representatives began the SALT I negotiations, with the intention of limiting each side's stockpile of nuclear weapons.

- The Nobel Peace Prize was awarded to the International Labour Organization (ILO), a Geneva, Switzerland–based organization devoted to workers' rights, labor reform and assistance to developing countries. Cited in the award: "ILO has permanently influenced the social welfare legislation of every single country."

Landmark US Events

Jan 20 Richard Nixon was sworn in as the 37th president of the United States.

Jan 28 A blowout on an oil platform located six miles off the California coast caused a massive oil

> What kind of nation we will be, what kind of world we will live in, whether we shape the future in the image of our hopes, is ours to determine by our actions and our choices. The greatest honor history can bestow is the title of peacemaker. This honor now beckons America—the chance to help lead the world at last out of the valley of turmoil, and onto that high ground of peace that man has dreamed of since the dawn of civilization. If we succeed, generations to come will say of us now living that we mastered our moment, that we helped make the world safe for mankind. This is our summons to greatness. I believe the American people are ready to answer this call.
> —from Richard Nixon's inaugural address

spill in the Santa Barbara Channel, contaminating the city's beaches and harbor. The blowout caused three million gallons of crude oil to contaminate the ocean (with a 35-mile oil slick)—it was the largest oil spill in American waters up to that time. The disaster prompted new environmental laws and regulations.

Mar 10 James Earl Ray pled guilty to the assassination of Martin Luther King, Jr.

Apr 9 At Harvard University, the administration building was seized by hundreds of students, mostly members of Students for a Democratic Society.

May 10 In Vietnam, the Battle of Hamburger Hill began.

May 15 Robert Rayford ("Robert R."), an American teenager from

Missouri, died of symptoms later attributed to HIV/AIDS.

June 22 A fire began on the polluted Cuyahoga River in northeast Ohio. While not the first conflagration of its type, media coverage and public outrage highlighted environmental concerns and eventually led to the Clean Water Act and the establishment of the Environmental Protection Agency.

June 23 Warren E. Burger was sworn in as chief justice of the United States.

June 28 The Stonewall Riots began at Greenwich Village, New York. Fed up with consistent police harassment of gay, lesbian, bisexual and transgendered people, hundreds of people gathered at the Stonewall Inn after a police raid. The ensuing days of protest would become a catalyst for the gay rights movement in the United States. See "Spotlight on American Anniversaries."

July 4 Darlene Ferrin and Michael Mageau were shot at Blue Rock Springs, CA, the second known victims of the Zodiac Killer. Mageau survived, but Ferrin died.

July 8 Following President Nixon's meeting with South Vietnamese President Nguyen Van Thieu on June 8, the first troop withdrawals of the Vietnam War begin.

July 18 Chappaquiddick Incident: Senator Edward Kennedy drove off a bridge at Chappaquiddick Island, MA. While Kennedy swam away and survived, he didn't report the accident for over ten hours, and his passenger, campaign worker Mary Jo Kopechne, died in the vehicle. The resulting scandal quashed Kennedy's intentions of a presidential run in 1972.

July 25 During a speech at Guam, President Nixon declared the Nixon Doctrine, or the expectation of US allies to manage their own defenses. The doctrine led to the "Vietnamization" of the Vietnam War.

Aug 8–9 At Los Angeles, members of the Manson Family murdered actress Sharon Tate and four others. The group's murderous activity would continue the next night, when Charles Manson and his followers murdered Leno and Rosemary LaBianca.

Aug 17 Hurricane Camille made landfall on the Mississippi coast. Generating winds of up to 175 miles per hour, the category 5 tropical cyclone was the second-most intense storm to ever hit the

United States. Camille killed 259 and caused damages of $1.43 billion.

Sept 5 US Army Lieutenant William Calley was charged with six counts of premeditated murder stemming from the 1968 My Lai Massacre in Vietnam.

Oct 8 Days of Rage: The Weathermen, a militant faction of Students for a Democratic Society, began a series of protests surrounding the "Chicago Eight" conspiracy trial at Chicago, IL. The trial and protests marked the continuing fallout from the violence and demonstrations at the 1968 Democratic National Convention.

Oct 15 The Moratorium to End the War in Vietnam began. Large demonstrations were held at Boston, London, and New York City. An estimated two million protesters took part.

Nov 3 "The Silent Majority": In a speech, President Richard Nixon appealed for support of his Vietnam policies to this large, unseen group, asking also that they deny the counterculture.

Nov 12 Independent investigative journalist Seymour Hersh broke the My Lai Massacre story to a national audience, ending the US military's media coverup of the event.

Nov 20 A large group of Native Americans seized Alcatraz Island at San Francisco, CA, occupying it for 19 months and stimulating a wave of support for Native American issues.

Dec 4 At Chicago, IL, Black Panther Party members Fred Hampton and Mark Clark were shot dead by Chicago Police.

Dec 27 The Weather Underground (WUO) began a series of meetings at Flint, MI ("The Flint War Council") with the purpose of disbanding the Students for a Democratic Society (SDS) and becoming an antigovernment guerilla organization.

Culture

Literary Arts

■ The Nobel Prize in Literature was awarded to Irishman Samuel Beckett: Beckett's pessimism "houses a love of mankind that grows in understanding as it plumbs further into the depths of abhorrence, a despair that has to reach the utmost bounds of suffering to discover that compassion has no bounds. From that position, in the realms of annihilation, rises the writing of Samuel Beckett like a miserere from all mankind, its muffled minor key sounding liberation to the oppressed, and comfort to those in need."

Fiction

June 16 *Newsday* journalist Mike McGrady and 24 colleagues perpetrated a literary hoax targeting the publishing industry—and the American public hungry for potboilers—when they authored *Naked Came the Stranger* by "Penelope Ashe." A novel chronicling the many sexual escapades of a Long Island housewife, *Naked Came the Stranger* was meant to show that any poorly written book with sex could sell. McGrady's office memo inviting participation read: "There will be an unremitting emphasis on sex. Also, true excellence in writing will be quickly blue-penciled into oblivion." Lyle Stuart sold 20,000 copies before the authors (including

Pulitzer Prize winners) revealed themselves on David Frost's television show. Thereafter, the novel sold 90,000 more copies. It is still in print.

■ *The Left Hand of Darkness*, by Ursula K. Le Guin

■ *Portnoy's Complaint*, by Philip Roth

■ *The Godfather*, by Mario Puzo

■ *Ada, or Ardor*, by Vladimir Nabokov

■ *I Sing the Body Electric*, by Ray Bradbury

■ *The Andromeda Strain*, by Michael Crichton

■ *The Four-Gated City*, by Doris Lessing, concluding volume of the "Children of Violence" quintet

■ *Slaughterhouse Five*, by Kurt Vonnegut

■ *The Poseidon Adventure*, by Paul Gallico

■ *Rich Man, Poor Man*, by Irwin Shaw

■ *Ubik*, by Philip K. Dick

■ *The French Lieutenant's Woman*, John Fowles

■ *Master and Commander*, by Patrick O'Brian

■ *The Promise*, by Chaim Potok

■ *Papillon*, by Henri Charrière

■ *Travels with My Aunt*, by Graham Green

■ *Runaway Horses*, by Yukio Mishima

■ *Jakob the Liar*, by Jurek Becker

■ *The Mephisto Waltz*, by Fred Mustard Stewart

Nonfiction

■ *I Know Why the Caged Bird Sings*, by Maya Angelou

- *On Death and Dying*, by Elisabeth Kübler-Ross

- *The Great Railway Bazaar: By Train Through Asia*, by Paul Theroux

- *Inside the Third Reich*, by Albert Speer

- *The 900 Days: The Siege of Leningrad*, by Harrison E. Salisbury

- *The Peter Principle*, by Laurence J. Peter and Raymond Hull

Children's Literature

- *The Very Hungry Caterpillar*, by Eric Carle

- *Sylvester and the Magic Pebble*, by William Steig (Caldecott Medal)

- *Charlotte Sometimes*, by Penelope Farmer

- *Sounder*, by William H. Armstrong

- *The Cay*, by Theodore Taylor

Theater and Opera

Mar 16 The musical *1776* opened at the 46th Street Theatre with William Daniels starring as John Adams, Ken Howard as Thomas Jefferson and Betty Buckley as Martha Jefferson. The show won three Tony Awards: Best Musical, Best Direction and Best Featured Actor (Ronald Holgate). Peter Stone wrote the book and Sherman Edwards composed the music and lyrics. It ran for 1,217 performances.

Dec 2 Muhammad Ali, suspended from boxing, made his Broadway debut in *Buck White*, a musical with only seven performances.

Film
Academy Awards for 1969
(Awarded in 1970)

- Best Picture: *Midnight Cowboy*— the first X-rated film to receive an Oscar

- Best Director: John Schlesinger, *Midnight Cowboy*

- Best Actor: John Wayne, *True Grit*

- Best Supporting Actor: Gig Young, *They Shoot Horses, Don't They?*

- Best Actress: Maggie Smith, *The Prime of Miss Jean Brodie*

- Best Supporting Actress: Goldie Hawn, *Cactus Flower*

- Burt Bacharach won Oscars in two categories: Best Original Score, for *Butch Cassidy and the Sundance Kid*; and Best Original Song, for "Raindrops Keep Fallin' On My Head" from *Butch Cassidy*, which he shared with lyricist Hal David.

Notable Films
- *Midnight Cowboy*
- *The Prime of Miss Jean Brodie*
- *They Shoot Horses, Don't They?*
- *Easy Rider*
- *Butch Cassidy and the Sundance Kid*
- *Anne of the Thousand Days*
- *True Grit*
- *Z*
- *Alice's Restaurant*
- *Hello, Dolly*
- *The Sterile Cuckoo*
- *The Wild Bunch*
- *Sweet Charity*
- *Bob & Carol & Ted & Alice*

Television

Jan 13 Dick York collapsed on the set of "Bewitched!" York's failing health led him to quit the show, ushering in the Dick Sargent era.

Apr 3 CBS canceled "The Smothers Brothers." This was the end result of the show's trend toward political satire and increased cultural comment.

June 3 "Star Trek" aired its final new episode ("Turnabout Intruder") after cancellation by NBC. The program would go on to worldwide fame in syndication.

July 20 Live, from the moon, it's . . . 720 million people around the world watched Neil Armstrong and Buzz Aldrin become the first humans to walk on the surface of the moon.

Premieres
- "Scooby-Do, Where Are You!"
- "Brady Bunch"
- "Monty Python's Flying Circus" (UK)
- "Sesame Street"
- "Hee Haw"
- "H.R. Pufnstuf"
- "The Courtship of Eddie's Father"
- "Marcus Welby, M.D."
- "Love, American Style"
- "The Benny Hill Show" (UK)

Music

Mar 1 Doors singer Jim Morrison was arrested for indecent exposure.

June 2 At their "Bed-In" held at Room 1742 at the Queen Elizabeth Hotel, Montreal, QC, Canada, John Lennon and Yoko Ono recorded the song "Give Peace a Chance," with support from hangers-on and friends, including Timothy Leary and Tom Smothers.

July 5 At Hyde Park, London, The Rolling Stones played a tribute concert to the recently deceased Brian Jones. Hundreds of thousands of fans attended. It was Mick Taylor's first performance with the group.

Aug 15 The Woodstock Music Festival began in upstate New York. See "Spotlight on American Anniversaries."

Aug 30–31 The Isle of Wight Festival, held at Wootton on the English island county, drew 150,000 music fans to see such acts as Bob Dylan, The Band, The Who, The Pretty Things and Joe Cocker.

Dec 6 300,000 fans swarmed the Altamont Motor Speedway at Northern California for a free festival featuring performances by The Flying Burrito Brothers; Santana; Jefferson Airplane; Crosby, Stills, Nash & Young; and headliners The Rolling Stones. The concert was marred by violence, including the death of Meredith Hunter, an African-American man who was beaten to death in the crowd by a member of the Hell's Angels motorcycle gang, who themselves were hired as security for the event.

Popular Songs

- The Beatles, "Come Together" and "Get Back" (with Billy Preston)
- The Rolling Stones, "Honky Tonk Women"
- Elvis Presley, "In the Ghetto" and "Suspicious Minds"
- The Isley Brothers, "It's Your Thing"
- The Archies, "Sugar Sugar"
- David Bowie, "Space Oddity"
- The 5th Dimension, "Aquarius/Let the Sunshine In"
- Johnny Cash, "A Boy Named Sue"
- The Temptations, "I Can't Get Next to You"
- Sly and the Family Stone, "Hot Fun in the Summertime"
- Tommy James & the Shondells, "Crystal Blue Persuasion"
- Marvin Gaye, "Too Busy Thinking About My Baby"
- Creedence Clearwater Revival, "Proud Mary"
- Neil Diamond, "Sweet Caroline"
- Blood, Sweat & Tears, "Spinning Wheel"
- Stevie Wonder, "My Cherie Amour"
- Oliver, "Good Morning Starshine"
- Jackie DeShannon, "Put a Little Love in Your Heart"
- Bob Dylan, "Lay Lady Lay"
- Glen Campbell, "Galveston"

Notable Albums

- *The Stooges*, by The Stooges
- *David Bowie*, by David Bowie

- *Abbey Road*, by The Beatles
- *Santana*, by Santana
- *Tommy*, by The Who
- *Led Zeppelin* and *Led Zeppelin II*, by Led Zeppelin
- *The Band*, by The Band
- *Clouds*, by Joni Mitchell
- *Let It Bleed*, by The Rolling Stones
- *In the Court of the Crimson King*, by King Crimson
- *Five Leaves Left*, by Nick Drake
- *Nashville Skyline*, by Bob Dylan
- *Dusty in Memphis*, by Dusty Springfield
- *The Gilded Palace of Sin*, by The Flying Burrito Brothers
- *At San Quentin*, by Johnny Cash
- *Cloud Nine* and *Puzzle People*, by The Temptations
- *The Age of Aquarius*, by The 5th Dimension
- *Beck-Ola*, by The Jeff Beck Band
- *Kick Out the Jams*, by MC5
- *Trout Mask Replica*, by Captain Beefheart

- *Ummagumma*, by Pink Floyd
- *Hot Rats*, by Frank Zappa
- *I Got Dem Ol' Kozmic Blues Again Mama!*, by Janis Joplin
- *Songs from a Room*, by Leonard Cohen
- *In a Silent Way*, by Miles Davis
- *Soul '69*, by Aretha Franklin
- *The Ballad of Easy Rider*, by The Byrds
- *Completely Well*, by B.B. King
- *Hot Buttered Soul*, by Isaac Hayes
- *Green Is Blues*, by Al Green
- *Fathers and Sons*, by Muddy Waters
- *David's Album*, by Joan Baez
- *Diana Ross Presents The Jackson 5*, by The Jackson 5
- *From Memphis to Vegas/From Vegas to Memphis*, by Elvis Presley
- *Easy*, by Marvin Gaye

Art

- *Flag (Moratorium)*, by Jasper Johns, a print commissioned by The Committee Against the War in Vietnam. The painting's colors refer to Agent Orange and camouflage: viewers fixedly looking at a white dot would "see" the regular red, white and blue US flag.
- After NASA invited him to watch the *Apollo* 11 launch, Robert Rauschenberg created the "Stoned Moon" lithographs.
- Salvador Dali designed the iconic label (still in use) for Chupa Chups, the Spanish lollipops.
- *Blue Green*, by Ellsworth Kelly, was commissioned by UNESCO for their headquarters.

- *Montauk* series, Willem de Kooning
- *Bestiaire et Musique*, by Marc Chagall
- *Grau*, Gerhard Richter

Science and Technology

Jan 14 The Soviet Union launched *Soyuz* 4 with cosmonaut Vladimir Shatalov aboard.

Jan 15 The Soviet Union launched *Soyuz* 5, with the expressed purpose of docking with *Soyuz* 4 while in orbit. The mission was the first-ever docking of two manned spacecraft while in orbit, and first-ever crew transfer from one space vehicle to another. This was achieved via spacewalk, or extra-vehicular activity (EVA).

Feb 24 *Mariner* 6 was launched from Cape Kennedy Air Force Station at Florida, followed by *Mariner* 7 (launched Mar 27). Together, these spacecraft provided new information about Mars, making flybys and taking photographs of features.

Apr 4 Surgeons Denton A. Cooley and Domingo Liotta achieved the first clinical implantation of an artificial heart inside the chest of a living patient.

May 18 *Apollo* 10 was launched as the fourth manned mission of the Apollo space program and a dress rehearsal for *Apollo* 11.

July 16 The *Apollo* 11 mission was launched from Kennedy Space Center at Merritt Island, FL. The historic spaceflight landed the first two humans on the surface of the moon. See "Spotlight on World Anniversaries."

Oct 17 William S. Boyle and George Smith created the first charge-coupled device (CCD) at AT&T Bell Labs. The technology remains a major component in digital imaging for cameras and medical devices.

Oct 29 The first message was sent over ARPANET, a major component of the early framework of the Internet.

Nov 14 *Apollo* 12 launched from Kennedy Space Center at Merritt Island, FL. It was the sixth manned spaceflight of the Apollo space program.

- The Nobel Prize in Physics was awarded to Murray Gell-Mann "for his contributions and discoveries concerning the classification of elementary particles and their interactions."
- The Nobel Prize in Chemistry was awarded to Derek H.R. Barton and Odd Hassel "for their contributions to the development of the concept of conformation and its application in chemistry."
- The Nobel Prize in Physiology or Medicine was awarded to Max Delbruck, Alfred D. Hershey and Salvador E. Luria "for their discoveries concerning the replication mechanism and the genetic structure of viruses."

Commerce and New Products

Feb 9 The Boeing 747 jet airliner made its first test flight.

Mar 2 The initial test flight of the Concorde was conducted at Toulouse, France.

Aug 18 Long John Silver's opened its first restaurant at Lexington, KY.

Aug 21 The first Gap store opened in San Francisco, CA. Its only product was Levi's jeans. Founded by Donald and Doris Fisher, the Gap expanded into a chain of stores in less than five years.

Oct 31 Wal-Mart Stores, Inc. was first incorporated.

Nov 15 Dave Thomas opened the first Wendy's restaurant at Columbus, OH.

■ The Sveriges Riksbank Prize in Economic Sciences in Memory of Alfred Nobel, established in 1968, was first awarded in 1969. Recipients were Ragnar Frisch and Jan Tinbergen, "for having developed and applied dynamic models for the analysis of economic processes."

■ Published this year was the business bestseller, *The Peter Principle*, by Laurence J. Peter and Raymond Hull, which explained that "every employee tends to rise to his level of incompetence."

Sports

Auto Racing

■ Daytona 500: LeeRoy Yarbrough

■ Indianapolis 500: Mario Andretti

■ Grand National NASCAR Cup winner: David Pearson

■ Formula One Drivers' Championship: Jackie Stewart (Matra International)

Baseball

Feb 4 Owners of the 24 Major League Baseball clubs elected Bowie Kuhn commissioner. MLB's fifth commissioner, Kuhn served until 1984.

Apr 7 Ted Williams made his debut as a major league baseball manager. The New York Yankees defeated his Washington Senators 8–4.

Apr 14 The first major league baseball game played outside the United States occurred as the Montreal Expos hosted the St. Louis Cardinals at Jarry Park in Canada. The Expos, a brand-new expansion team, won 8–7.

June 8 The New York Yankees honored Mickey Mantle by retiring his number 7 in a ceremony preceding a doubleheader against the Chicago White Sox.

Aug 5 Willie Stargell of the Pittsburgh Pirates hit the only home run ever out of Dodger Stadium. His blast off pitcher Alan Foster cleared the right-field pavilion and traveled an estimated 506 feet from home plate.

Sept 22 Willie Mays of the San Francisco Giants hit the 600th home run of his career, a pinch-hit homer against Mike Corkins of the San Diego Padres.

Oct 4 Following the inauguration of divisional play in the MLB, National League and American League teams opened competition in the first League Championship Series. The New York Mets beat the Atlanta Braves, 9–5 in the opening game of the NLCS, while the Baltimore Orioles defeated the Minnesota Twins 4–3 (in 12 innings) in the first ALCS game.

Oct 11–16 In the World Series, New York's "Miracle Mets" defeated the Baltimore Orioles four games to one.

Basketball

■ NBA Finals: The Boston Celtics defeated the Los Angeles Lakers four games to three.

Football

Jan 12 Super Bowl III: The New York Jets of the American Football League beat the Baltimore Colts of the National Football League 16–7, overcoming their 17-point underdog status and vindicating quarterback Joe Namath's brash guarantee of a win. It was the first professional football championship to bear the "Super Bowl" title.

■ Rose Bowl: USC Trojans 10, Michigan Wolverines 3

■ Orange Bowl: Penn State Nittany Lions 10, Missouri Tigers 3

■ Sugar Bowl: Mississippi Rebels 27, Arkansas Razorbacks 22

■ Cotton Bowl: Texas Longhorns 21, Notre Dame Fighting Irish 17

■ The Heisman Trophy was won by Oklahoma running back Steve Owens, who rushed for 3,867 yards and scored 56 touchdowns in three seasons with the Sooners.

■ The 1969 college football season was commemorated by the NCAA as the 100th anniversary of the first-ever college football game, the 1869 game between Rutgers and Princeton. Many teams wore a specially designed decal on their helmets that featured the number "100" inside the outline of a football.

Golf

■ The Masters: George Archer

■ US Open: Orville Moody

■ Open Championship: Tony Jacklin

■ PGA Championship: Raymond Floyd

Hockey

Feb 16 Detroit Red Wings center Alex Delvecchio became the third player in NHL history to accumulate 1,000 regular-season points.

Mar 2 Phil Esposito, center of the Boston Bruins, became the first player in National Hockey League history to tally 100 points in a season when he scored a goal in

Boston's 4–0 victory over the Pittsburgh Penguins.

Apr 27–May 4 Stanley Cup: The Montreal Canadiens defeated the St. Louis Blues in four straight games.

Horse Racing

Feb 22 Barbara Jo Rubin became the first woman jockey to win a thoroughbred horse race in the United States. She rode Cohesion to victory by a neck over Reely Beeg in the ninth race at Charles Town Race Track in West Virginia.

May 3 Majestic Prince, ridden by Johnny Longden, won the Kentucky Derby and Preakness Stakes (May 17).

June 7 Belmont Stakes: Arts and Letters, ridden by Braulio Baeza.

■ Arts and Letters would be named 1969 Horse of the Year.

Soccer

Apr 26 Manchester City defeated Leicester City 1–0 in the F.A. Cup.

Tennis

■ US Open: Australian Rod Laver defeated fellow countryman Tony Roche in four sets to complete the second grand slam of his career. In women's singles play, Margaret Court defeated Nancy Richey 6–2 6–2.

■ Wimbledon: In men's singles, Australian Rod Laver defeated fellow countryman John Newcombe 6–4 5–7 6–4 6–4. In women's singles play, Great Britain's Ann Jones defeated Billie Jean King of the United States 3–6 6–3 6–2.

1969 Deaths

■ Irene Castle, English dancer and stage star

■ Edward Victor ("Eddie") Cicotte, American baseball player banned due to his participation in the Black Sox Scandal of 1919

■ Bud Collyer, American radio personality

■ Ivy Compton-Burnett, English author

■ Maureen ("Little Mo") Catherine Connolly, American tennis player

■ Otto Dix, German artist

■ Allen Dulles, American diplomat who headed the CIA

■ Harley Earl, automobile designer and executive (General Motors)

■ Dwight D. Eisenhower, 34th president of the United States

■ Levi Eshkol, Israeli prime minister

■ George Murphy ("Pops") Foster, American jazz musician

■ Judy Garland, American actress and singer

■ Vito Genovese, Italian-American mobster—the "Boss of all Bosses"

■ Walter Gropius, German architect (founder of the Bauhaus School)

■ Walter Hagen, American golfer

■ Coleman Hawkins, American jazz saxophonist

■ George ("Gabby") Hayes, American character actor

■ Sonja Henie, Norwegian Olympic figure skater and film star

■ Conrad Hilton, Jr, American scion of the hotel family

■ Daisy and Violet Hilton, English conjoined twins in the entertainment business

■ Ho Chi Minh, Vietnamese revolutionary leader

- Jeffrey Hunter, American actor

- Brian Jones, English musician, founder of The Rolling Stones

- Boris Karloff (William Henry Pratt), English actor famous for portraying Frankenstein's creature

- Joseph P. Kennedy, American businessman, investor and politician

- Jack Kerouac, American "Beat" writer

- Rod La Rocque, American actor

- Frank Loesser, American songwriter ("Baby, It's Cold Outside" and "What Are You Doing New Year's Eve?")

- Madhubala (Mumtaz Jehan Begum Dehlavi), Indian actress, superstar of Indian cinema

- Rocky Marciano, American boxer

- Leo McCarey, American filmmaker

- Howard McNear, American actor ("The Andy Griffith Show")

- Ludwig Mies van der Rohe, German-American architect

- Frank Joseph ("Lefty") O'Doul, American baseball player, manager and executive

- Cecil Frank Powell, British physicist, Nobel Laureate

- Pee Wee Russell, American jazz musician

- Benjamin Shahn, Lithuanian-American artist

- Otto Stern, German physicist, Nobel Laureate

- Sharon Tate, American actress

- Charles B. ("Chuck") Taylor, American Basketball Hall of Famer

- Robert Taylor, American actor

- Kam Tong, Chinese-American actor

- John Kennedy Toole, American author (*A Confederacy of Dunces*)

- Leonard Woolf, English publisher (Hogarth) and author

- John Wyndham, English author (*Day of the Triffids*)

1994

25 YEARS AGO

Landmark World Events

Jan 1 NAFTA, the North American Free Trade Agreement, went into effect. The pact established a trilateral free trade zone between Mexico, Canada and the United States.

Jan 14 US President Bill Clinton and Russian President Boris Yeltsin signed the Kremlin Accords. The agreements stopped the pre-programmed targeting of nuclear weapons at targets by any nation. Russia also agreed to dismantle its nuclear stockpile in Ukraine.

Feb 25 Israeli medical doctor Baruch Goldstein opened fire inside the Cave of the Patriarchs at Hebron, killing 29 Muslims at prayer before being subdued and beaten to death by worshippers.

Mar 12 The Church of England ordained female priests for the first time.

Mar 23 Mexican presidential candidate Luis Donaldo Colosio was assassinated at Tijuana.

Mar 27 In Italy, media baron Silvio Berlusconi's right-wing coalition won the general election.

Apr 6 The plane carrying Rwandan President Juvenal Habyarimana and Cyprien Ntaryamira, President of Burundi, was shot down over Kigali, Rwanda. Habyarimana's assassination sparked ethnic tensions in Rwanda, leading to the Rwandan genocide. Between Apr 7 and July 15, 500,000 to almost one million ethnic Tutsi and Pygmy Batwa Rwandans were slaughtered by the majority Hutu government.

Apr 26 China Airlines Flight 140 crashed on approach to Nagoya Airport at Japan, killing 264 passengers and 15 crewmembers aboard. Seven people survived.

May 6 The Channel Tunnel opened. The rail tunnel links Folkstone, Kent, England, with Coquelles, Pas-de-Calais, France, 250 feet under the bed of the English Channel. Passenger service on

the undersea railway began Nov 14.

May 10 Nelson Mandela was inaugurated in South Africa. He became the country's first black president.

May 22 Pope John Paul II issued an Apostolic letter reestablishing the Catholic Church's position requiring only men to be priests.

June 27 A nighttime sarin gas attack perpetrated by the Aum Shinrikyo cult at Matsumoto, Japan, killed eight and injured hundreds.

July 8 North Korean president Kim Il Sung died of a heart attack at 82. He was succeeded by his son, Kim Jong Il.

Aug 31 The Provisional Irish Republican Army announced the complete cessation of military operations.

Sept 28 The car ferry MS *Estonia* sank in the Baltic Sea while en route from Tallinn, Estonia, to Sweden. 852 people were killed in the second-worst peacetime maritime disaster in European history after the sinking of the *Titanic*.

Oct 26 Israel and Jordan signed peace accords to begin an end to the nearly 50-year state of war between the two countries.

Nov 28 Via referendum, Norwegian voters decided against joining the European Union.

Dec 1 Ernesto Zedillo took office as the president of Mexico.

Dec 11 Russian troops deployed to Chechnya, beginning the First Chechen War.

Dec 14 Construction began on the Three Gorges Dam at Sandouping, China.

Dec 19 The planned exchange rate correction of the Mexican peso to the US dollar went haywire, triggering a global financial crisis and a multibillion-dollar bailout by the US government.

■ Nobel Peace Prize: Yasser Arafat, Shimon Peres and Yitzhak Rabin, "for their efforts to create peace in the Middle East"

Landmark US Events

Jan 6 American figure skater Nancy Kerrigan was struck on the knee with an iron rod at Cobo Arena in Detroit, MI, where she had been practicing for the upcoming US Figure Skating Championships.

Jan 17 The Northridge earthquake struck the Los Angeles metro area, killing 57 and injuring thousands.

Jan 25 In his State of the Union address, President Bill Clinton called for gun control, including a ban on assault weapons, the widespread reform of welfare and healthcare programs and a "three strikes" law for violent repeat offenders.

Feb 22 Aldrich Ames, a veteran CIA counterintelligence analyst, was charged along with his wife of spying for the Soviet Union and Russia. Ames was later convicted and is serving a life term in prison.

Mar 3 The last US troops withdrew from Somalia, effectively ending the United Nations Operation in Somalia II (UNOSOM II), which had begun in 1993 and included the Battle of Mogadishu.

Mar 27 A series of violent tornadoes in the southeastern United States killed 40 people, injured hundreds and caused almost $150 million in damages.

Apr 22 Former president Richard Nixon died at 81 from a severe stroke.

May 10 The state of Illinois executed serial killer John Wayne Gacy by lethal injection. Gacy

🔍 The Kerrigan Attack

Just after training on Jan 6, 1994, American figure skater Nancy Kerrigan was attacked and injured by a man with an iron bar, plunging the nation in a frenzy of speculation before the upcoming US Figure Skating Championships and Winter Olympics. At the US Championships, the contest winner was Tonya Harding, who was later accused, along with her ex-husband, Jeff Gillooly, and three others, of planning and carrying out the attack. Kerrigan recovered in time to participate in the Winter Olympics at Lillehammer, Norway, in February, winning a silver medal. Harding came in eighth, suffering a broken lace and later a fall. In plea bargaining, Gillooly admitted his role in the attack and testified that Harding had been involved in the planning. Her bodyguard and two others were later indicted, and Harding was put on two years' probation. Harding also was stripped of her US title and banned from the US Figure Skating Association for life.

The Gingrich Revolution

United nationally behind the messaging of Congressman Newt Gingrich (R-GA), Republicans running in the midterm elections Nov 8 conducted an all-out assault on President Bill Clinton, hammering away at him as a "tax-and-spend liberal" and uniting themselves under Gingrich's "Contract with America" banner. The intention was to reduce federal taxation, balance the federal budget and deconstruct federal welfare programs that had been in place since the New Deal. Republicans gained 54 seats in the House and eight seats in the Senate, giving them control of both houses, and Gingrich ascended to the House Speaker chair. With Gingrich as Speaker and Bob Dole installed as Senate Majority Leader, the 104th United States Congress enacted every bill associated with the Contract with America. Only President Clinton's veto pen stood in the way of Gingrich and the Republicans' newly gained power.

killed more than 30 men and boys.

May 19 Jacqueline Kennedy Onassis, former first lady of the United States, died of cancer at the age of 64.

June 13 Nicole Brown Simpson, ex-wife of O.J. Simpson, and Ron Goldman were found murdered in front of Simpson's townhouse.

June 17 O.J. Simpson was arrested in connection with the murder of his ex-wife, Nicole Brown Simpson, and Ronald Goldman. Simpson had fled his home in the morning rather than be arrested. Later that evening, he and his friend Al Cowlings were in Simpson's white Ford Bronco. After leading police on a lengthy low-speed car chase over Los Angeles's freeways, the pair eventually arrived back at Simpson's home, where he was apprehended. The drama was carried live on television nationwide; an estimated 90 million people watched.

Sept 8 USAir Flight 427 crashed on approach to Pittsburgh International Airport due to catastrophic rudder malfunction. All 127 passengers and five crew members aboard were killed.

Sept 12 Frank Eugene Corder, an itinerant truck driver from Maryland, crashed a stolen Cessna 150 into the South Lawn of the White House in an apparent attempt to hit the building. He was the only casualty.

Sept 13 President Clinton signed the Assault Weapons Ban into law. It restricted civilian ownership of semi-automatic firearms and large-capacity ammunition magazines.

Sept 13 President Clinton signed into law the Violence against Women Act. It funded the investigation and prosecution of violent crimes against women and imposed automatic and mandatory restitution on the convicted. The bill was sponsored by Senator Joe Biden (D-DE) and New York State Representative Louise Slaughter.

Sept 19 Operation Uphold Democracy: With authorization from the United Nations Security Council, elements of the US military began entering Haiti with a mission to reinstate President Jean-Bertrand Aristide, who had been deposed in 1991 during a military coup d'état.

Nov 28 Serial killer Jeffrey Dahmer and murderer Jesse Anderson were bludgeoned to death inside Columbia Correctional Institution at Portage, WI, by fellow inmate and convicted murderer Christopher Scarver.

■ The Whitewater Scandal: Decades-old documents concerning Bill and Hillary Clinton's financial dealings with Whitewater Development Corporation become the basis of an inquiry by the US Judiciary Committee and its special counsel, Kenneth Starr.

Culture

Literary Arts

■ The Nobel Prize in Literature was awarded to Kenzaburo Oe.

Fiction

■ *Disclosure*, by Michael Crichton

■ *The Chamber*, by John Grisham

■ *The Ice Storm*, by Rick Moody

■ *Accident* and *The Gift*, by Danielle Steel

■ *Remember Me*, by Mary Higgins Clark

■ *Insomnia*, by Stephen King

■ *Captain Corelli's Mandolin*, by Louis de Bernieres

■ *The Concrete Blonde*, by Michael Connelly

- *Life After God*, by Douglas Coupland
- *The Alienist*, by Caleb Carr
- *Snow Falling on Cedars*, by David Guterson
- *Debt of Honor*, by Tom Clancy

Nonfiction

- *Midnight in the Garden of Good and Evil*, by John Berendt
- *Prozac Nation*, by Elizabeth Wurtzel
- *Long Walk to Freedom*, by Nelson Mandela
- *The Hot Zone: The Terrifying True Story of the Origins of the Ebola Virus*, by Richard Preston
- *Songs My Mother Taught Me*, by Marlon Brando
- *Images: My Life in Film*, by Ingmar Bergman
- *Last Train to Memphis: The Rise of Elvis Presley*, by Peter Guralnick
- *The Late Shift: Letterman, Leno, and the Network Battle for the Night*, by Bill Carter
- *A Drinking Life: A Memoir*, by Pete Hamill

Children's Literature

- *Guess How Much I Love You*, by Sam McBratney with art by Anita Jeram
- *Catherine, Called Birdy*, by Karen Cushman

Theater and Opera

May 9 Stephen Sondheim's *Passion* opened at the Plymouth Theatre and garnered four 1994 Tony Awards, including Best Musical, Best Book, Best Score and Best Actress (Donna Murphy).

Nov 17 *Sunset Boulevard*, a musical retelling of the famed Billy Wilder film, opened at the Minskoff Theatre. A popular and critical success, it netted seven 1995 Tony Awards, including Best Musical, Best Book, Best Score and Best Actress (Glenn Close as Norma Desmond). It ran for 976 performances, until Mar 22, 1997.

Film

Academy Awards for 1994
(Awarded in 1995)

- Best Picture: *Forrest Gump*
- Best Director: Robert Zemeckis, *Forrest Gump*
- Best Actor: Tom Hanks, *Forrest Gump*
- Best Supporting Actor: Martin Landau, *Ed Wood*
- Best Actress: Jessica Lange, *Blue Sky*
- Best Supporting Actress: Dianne Wiest, *Bullets over Broadway*

Notable Films

- *Forrest Gump*
- *Pulp Fiction*
- *The Lion King*
- *Little Women*
- *True Lies*
- *The Mask*
- *Speed*
- *Dumb and Dumber*
- *Four Weddings and a Funeral*
- *Interview with the Vampire*
- *Clear and Present Danger*
- *Ed Wood*
- *Quiz Show*
- *Reality Bites*
- *The House of the Spirits*
- *The Crow*
- *Wyatt Earp*
- *Angels in the Outfield*
- *The Client*
- *Three Colors: Red*
- *Hoop Dreams*
- *Blue Sky*
- *The Shawshank Redemption*
- *Bullets over Broadway*
- *Stargate*
- *The Santa Clause*
- *Legends of the Fall*
- *Nobody's Fool*
- *The Madness of King George*
- *The Adventures of Priscilla, Queen of the Desert*

Television

Mar 31 Appearing on the "Late Show with David Letterman," Madonna went on a profanity-laden tirade that became one of the most-censored events in American TV history.

Apr 14 Turner Classic Movies (TCM) made its debut.

Apr 28 "The Simpsons" broadcast its 100th episode on Fox.

May 13 Johnny Carson appeared as a surprise guest on the "Late Show with David Letterman," delivering a Top 10 List. It was Carson's last television appearance.

May 23 "Star Trek: The Next Generation" ended its television run after seven seasons.

June 1 FX, the first cable television network owned by Fox, made its debut.

June 17 DirecTV, the direct broadcast satellite service, made its debut.

Premieres

- "ER"
- "Touched by an Angel"
- "Friends"
- "Babylon 5"
- "Where on Earth Is Carmen Sandiego?"
- "Ellen"
- "Inside the Actor's Studio"
- "My So-Called Life"
- "Extra"
- "New York Undercover"
- "Party of Five"
- "Chicago Hope"

Radio

Nov 7 University of North Carolina at Chapel Hill college radio station WXYC became the first station to broadcast a continuous, free live stream over the Internet.

Music

Apr 5 Kurt Cobain, songwriter and frontman of the alternative

rock trio Nirvana, was found dead in his Seattle, WA, home from an apparent suicide.

Aug 12–14 Woodstock '94 began at Saugerties, NY, with performances by Nine Inch Nails, Aerosmith, Metallica, The Cranberries, Bob Dylan, Green Day and Crosby, Stills & Nash. Over 500,000 fans attended the event, which celebrated the 25th anniversary of the first Woodstock in 1969.

Nov 30 Rapper Tupac Shakur was shot five times and robbed while entering the lobby of Quad Recording Studios at Manhattan, New York City. Shakur survived the attack, only to be killed in a drive-by shooting two years later in 1996.

Popular Songs

- Bruce Springsteen, "Streets of Philadelphia"
- Rednex, "Cotton Eye Joe"
- All-4-One, "I Swear"
- Maria Carey, "Without You"
- Bryan Adams, Rod Stewart and Sting, "All for Love"
- Sheryl Crow, "All I Wanna Do"
- Mariah Carey, "All I Want for Christmas Is You"
- Ace of Base, "All That She Wants"
- Nirvana, "About a Girl (Unplugged)"
- The Cranberries, "Zombie"
- John Mellencamp and Me'shell Ndegeocello, "Wild Night"
- Green Day, "When I Come Around" and "Basket Case"
- Snoop Doggy Dogg, "What's My Name" and "Gin & Juice"
- Oasis, "Supersonic" and "Live Forever"
- Collective Soul, "Shine"
- Nine Inch Nails, "Closer"
- Elton John, "Can You Feel the Love Tonight" and "Circle of Life"
- Soundgarden, "Black Hole Sun"
- The Offspring, "Come Out and Play"
- Boyz II Men, "On Bended Knee"
- Beastie Boys, "Sabotage"
- Veruca Salt, "Seether"
- Brandy, "I Wanna Be Down"
- The Pretenders, "I'll Stand by You"
- Ini Kamoze, "Here Comes the Hotstepper"
- Coolio, "Fantastic Voyage"
- Smashing Pumpkins, "Disarm"
- TLC, "Creep"
- Aerosmith, "Crazy"
- Weezer, "Buddy Holly"
- Pearl Jam, "Better Man"

Notable Albums

- *The Lion King: Original Motion Picture Soundtrack*
- *Tuesday Night Music Club*, by Sheryl Crow
- *Under the Pink*, by Tori Amos
- *Dookie*, by Green Day
- *Mellow Gold*, by Beck
- *Live at the Acropolis*, by Yanni
- *Hoist*, by Phish
- *The Division Bell*, by Pink Floyd

- *Smash*, by The Offspring
- *Illmatic*, by Nas
- *Parklife*, by Blur
- *American Recordings*, by Johnny Cash
- *Southernplayalisticadillacmuzik*, by Outkast
- *Weezer*, by Weezer
- *Ill Communication*, by Beastie Boys
- *Regulate . . . G Funk Era*, by Warren G
- *Age Ain't Nothing but a Number*, by Aaliyah
- *Cracked Rear View*, by Hootie & the Blowfish
- *Voodoo Lounge*, by The Rolling Stones
- *Dummy*, by Portishead
- *Rhythm of Love*, by Anita Baker
- *Definitely Maybe*, by Oasis
- *II*, by Boyz II Men
- *Usher*, by Usher
- *Ready to Die*, by The Notorious B.I.G.
- *Brandy*, by Brandy
- *Monster*, by R.E.M.
- *Under the Table and Dreaming*, by Dave Matthews Band
- *No Need to Argue*, by The Cranberries
- *Korn*, by Korn
- *MTV Unplugged in New York*, by Nirvana
- *Wildflowers*, by Tom Petty
- *CrazySexyCool*, by TLC
- *My Life*, by Mary J. Blige
- *Vitalogy*, by Pearl Jam

Art

Feb 12 At the National Gallery, Oslo, Norway, one version of Edvard Munch's *The Scream* was stolen—on the same day that the Lillehammer Winter Olympic Games opened. The artwork was recovered on May 7.

- After more than a decade of restoration work, Michelangelo's fresco *The Last Judgement* was reopened for public view at the Sistine Chapel, Vatican City.

- *The World's First Collaborative Sentence*, by Douglas Davis. An ongoing textual and graphic online "performance," the work anticipated the blog and online posting era. Now a part of the Whitney Museum of American Art, it was originally hosted on the website of Lehman College as part of a 1994 retrospective of Davis's work.

- Kansai International Airport at Osaka, Japan opened. Designed by Italian architect and engineer Renzo Piano, its Terminal 1 was the longest building in the world.

- *Spider*, monumental bronze sculpture by Louise Bourgeois

- *Lesende* (*Reader*) paintings, by Gerhard Richter

- *Away from the Flock*, a sheep in a tank of formaldehyde, by Damien Hirst

Science and Technology

Jan 1 Rasmus Lerdorf began work on PHP, or Hypertext Preprocessor, a computer language designed for creating dynamic web pages.

Jan 8 *Soyuz* TM-18 launched from Baikonur Cosmodrome at Kazakhstan, an enclave of Russia, with three cosmonauts aboard. One of them, Valeri Polyakov, would eventually spend 437.7 days in orbit on the *Mir* space station, a record for the longest stay in space by a human.

Jan 11 The Superhighway Summit was held at UCLA. The conference brought together leaders in government, industry and academia to discuss the dissemination of information in the Internet age. "We have a dream for . . . an information superhighway that can save lives, create jobs and give every American, young and old, the chance for the best education available to anyone, anywhere," Vice President Al Gore said in his keynote address. The term "information superhighway" had been used before and is usually credited to Gore.

Oct 1 Computer scientist Tim Berners-Lee founded the World Wide Web Consortium ("W3C") at the Massachusetts Institute of Technology. The group was tasked with developing common protocols for the World Wide Web (which Berners-Lee had already invented), thereby fostering its unified evolution.

Oct 10 Hakon Wium Lee first proposed the computer language concept of Cascading Style Sheets, or CSS.

Oct 13 NASA lost radio contact with the Magellan robotic space probe when it was presumably vaporized in the thick atmosphere of Venus, its target planet.

- The Nobel Prize in Physics was awarded "for pioneering contributions to the development of neutron scattering techniques for studies of condensed matter" to Bertram N. Brockhouse "for the development of neutron spectroscopy" and to Clifford G. Shull "for the development of the neutron diffraction technique."

■ The Nobel Prize in Chemistry was awarded to George A. Olah "for his contribution to carbocation chemistry."

■ The Nobel Prize in Physiology or Medicine was awarded to Alfred G. Gilman and Martin Rodbell "for their discovery of G-proteins and the role of these proteins in signal transduction in cells."

Commerce and New Products

Jan 1 The company that would become Yahoo! was founded by Stanford University graduate students Jerry Yang and David Filo.

Mar 7 Intel introduced the second generation of its Pentium microprocessor.

Apr 29 Commodore Computers declared bankruptcy.

Mar 5 CNET, a technology news website, was founded by Halsey Minor and Shelby Bonnie.

May 16 Apple Computer introduced the PowerBook 500 series of Macintosh portable computers.

Aug 16 IBM introduced the Simon Personal Communicator, a first-of-its-kind handheld touchscreen PDA. It was promptly overtaken by flip phones.

Oct 27 The first banner ad was sold to AT&T, which began to run the first Internet ad campaign.

Dec 15 Netscape introduced Navigator, its proprietary web browser.

■ The Sveriges Riksbank Prize in Economic Sciences in Memory of Alfred Nobel was awarded to John C. Harsanyi, John F. Nash, Jr, and Reinhard Seiten "for their pioneering analysis of equilibria in the theory of non-cooperative games."

■ In 1994, America Online reached one million subscribers, and for the first time there was widespread consumer access to the World Wide Web.

Sports

Auto Racing

May 1 Three-time Formula One champion Ayrton Senna was killed in an accident at San Marino Grand Prix at Imola, Italy.

■ Indianapolis 500: Al Unser, Jr

■ Daytona 500: Sterling Martin

■ Formula One Drivers' Championship: Michael Schumacher

Lillehammer 1994

The games of the XVII Winter Olympiad were held Feb 12 to Feb 27 at Lillehammer, Norway. It was the first winter games to be held separately from the summer games, and Lillehammer was the northernmost city to ever host an Olympic event. Sixty-seven nations participated, including nine former Soviet republics. Czech Republic and Slovakia's athletes competed separately for the first time, and Bosnia and Herzegovina debuted at the games after achieving their independence from Yugoslavia. Russia led the gold medal haul with 11, and won 23 medals overall, while host nation Norway led the cumulative medal count with 26.

Men's downhill skier Tommy Moe, Diann Roffe in women's super-G, Bonnie Blair in the women's 500 meter and 1,000 meter speed skating events, and Dan Jansen in men's 1,000 meter speed skating all captured gold for the United States. Blair, of Champaign, IL, became the first speed skater to win a gold medal in the same event in three consecutive Olympic Games when she won the 500 meter. With her Feb 23 victory in the 1,000 meter, she totaled five gold medals, more than any other American female athlete. Picabo Street (women's downhill), Nancy Kerrigan (figure skating), and Elizabeth McIntyre (women's moguls) won silver medals for the United States, which totaled 13 medals in all, good for fifth place.

Short track speed skating, a comparatively new discipline after its debut at the 1992 Winter Olympics, was dominated by South Korea, who won four of the six events. Sweden took home gold in ice hockey after tying the gold medal game with two minutes to play. After five rounds of shootout action resulted in a tie and one round of misses by both sides' players, it was Sweden's Peter Forsberg's score on Canadian goaltender Corey Hirsch in the seventh round that proved to be the gold medal difference.

Baseball

July 8 Boston Red Sox shortstop John Valentin recorded the 11th triple play in major league history in a game against the Seattle Mariners. In the sixth inning, Valentin caught a line drive hit by Marc Newfield, stepped on second base to double Mike Blowers and tapped Keith Mitchell before he could return to first.

Aug 12 Striking Major League Baseball players walked off the job, beginning the work stoppage that would last for 232 days. It was the eighth work stoppage in baseball history and was the culmination of years of acrimony that pitted the players and their union against the team owners. At the time of the strike, most clubs had played 113 games. With the sudden suspension of play, the entire 1994 postseason was lost, players having MVP seasons (like Frank Thomas of the Chicago White Sox and Ken Griffey, Jr, of the Seattle Mariners) hung up their cleats, and entire teams playing historic seasons (like the cursed Montreal Expos) saw their chance to make baseball history cut short.

Basketball

Jan 17 The Los Angeles (Northridge) earthquake forced postponement of a scheduled NBA game between the Lakers and the Sacramento Kings at the Great Western Forum. Earthquake damage forced the Clippers to move a pair of games from the Los Angeles Sports Arena. Their Jan 21 game against the Cleveland Cavaliers was played at the Forum, and their Jan 27 game against the New York Knicks was moved to The Pond at Anaheim.

Jan 30 The Boston Celtics retired No. 32, the jersey worn by forward Kevin McHale for 13 seasons.

Apr 16 Don Nelson became the seventh coach in American professional basketball history to win 800 games when his Golden State Warriors defeated the Utah Jazz 109–105.

■ NBA Finals: The Houston Rockets defeated the New York Knicks four games to three.

■ NCAA Division I Men's Basketball Tournament: Arkansas defeated Duke 76–72 to capture its first national championship.

Football

■ Super Bowl XXVIII: The Dallas Cowboys defeated the Buffalo Bills 30–13. The game was a rematch of the previous year's Super Bowl, and the Bills' fourth consecutive appearance in the championship game.

■ Orange Bowl: Nebraska 24, Miami 17l

■ Cotton Bowl: USC 55, Texas Tech 14

■ Sugar Bowl: Florida State 23, Florida 17

■ Rose Bowl: Penn State 38, Oregon 20

■ Fiesta Bowl: Colorado 41, Notre Dame 24

■ Heisman Trophy: Rashaan Salaam, running back for the University of Colorado

■ The NFL announced The Jacksonville Jaguars as its 30th franchise.

Golf

■ The Masters: Jose Maria Olazabal

■ US Open: Ernie Els won after Colin Montgomerie was defeated in an 18-hole playoff and Loren Roberts fell short on a second sudden-death hole. The 1994 US Open was golf legend Arnold Palmer's last major tournament as a participant.

■ Open Championship: Nick Price

■ PGA Championship: Nick Price

Hockey

Jan 8 Right wing Dino Ciccarelli of the Detroit Red Wings became the 19th player in NHL history to score 500 regular-season goals.

May 31–June 14 Stanley Cup: The New York Rangers defeated the Vancouver Canucks four games to three.

Horse Racing

■ Go for Gin, ridden by Chris McCarron, won the Kentucky Derby.

■ Tabasco Cat, ridden by Pat Day, won the Preakness Stakes and Belmont Stakes.

Soccer

May 14 Manchester United defeated Chelsea 4–0 in the F.A. Cup.

June 17–July 17 The FIFA World Cup was played in the United States for the first time. Held every four years, the 1994 games began in Chicago, IL, with a match between Germany and Bolivia and ended in Los Angeles, CA, with a final between Brazil and Italy on July 17. Brazil won in a penalty shootout 3–2. The games were watched on television by billions of fans around the world.

July 2 Andres Escobar, 27, a defender on Colombia's 1994 World Cup team, was shot 12 times and killed by an unknown assailant at Medellin, Colombia. The shooting occurred ten days after Escobar had scored an "own goal," accidentally kicking the ball into his own net in a 2–1 opening round upset loss to the United States. Witnesses said the shooter shouted "Goal! Goal!" as he fired each shot.

Tennis

■ US Open: In men's singles, Andre Agassi defeated Michael Stich 6–1 7–6 7–5. In women's singles action, Arantxa Sanchez Vicario of Spain defeated Germany's Steffi Graf 1–6 7–6 6–4.

■ Wimbledon Championships: In men's singles, Pete Sampras defeated Goran Ivanisevic 7–6 7–6 6–0. In women's singles action, Conchita Martinez of Spain defeated Martina Navratilova 6–4 3–6 6–3.

1994 Deaths

■ Claude Akins, American actor

■ Pierre Boulle, French author (*Bridge on the River Kwai, Planet of the Apes*)

■ Rossano Brazzi, Italian actor

■ Charles Bukowski, German-American poet and author

■ Matt Busby, Scottish soccer player and manager (Manchester United)

■ Cab (Cabell) Calloway, American bandleader, composer and actor

■ John Candy, Canadian comedian and actor

■ Macdonald Carey, American actor

■ James Clavell, bestselling Anglo-American novelist and screenwriter

■ Kurt Cobain, American musician

■ Elias Canetti, Bulgarian author, received 1981 Nobel Prize in Literature

■ William Conrad, American actor and voiceover artist

■ Joseph Cotten, American actor

■ John Curry, English Olympic figure skater

■ Peter Cushing, English actor

■ Ralph Ellison, American author (*Invisible Man*) and critic

■ Erich Honecker, East German political leader

■ Eugène Ionesco, Romanian playwright

■ Derek Jarman, English filmmaker

■ Donald Judd, American artist and furniture designer

■ Raul Julia, Puerto Rican actor

■ Kim Il Sung, North Korean dictator

■ Jack Kirby, comic book creator

■ Burt Lancaster, American actor

■ Walter Lantz, American animator, creator of Woody Woodpecker

■ Henry Mancini, American composer

■ Carmen McRae, American jazz singer

■ Melina Mercouri, Greek actress and politician

■ Harry Nilsson, American singer and songwriter

■ Richard Nixon, 37th president of the United States

■ Jacqueline Kennedy Onassis, former US first lady, editor

- Tip O'Neill, American politician, former US Speaker of the House

- John Osborne, English playwright

- Linus Pauling, American chemist

- George Peppard, American actor

- Karl Popper, Austrian philosopher

- Martha Raye, American actress and comedian

- Fernando Rey, Spanish actor

- Gilbert Roland, Mexican actor

- Cesar Romero, Cuban-American actor, played the Joker on "Batman"

- Wilma Rudolph, American Olympic sprinter

- Dean Rusk, US secretary of state (1961–69)

- Dick Sargent, American actor ("Bewitched")

- Telly Savalas, American actor ("Kojak")

- Richard Scarry, American children's author

- Randy Shilts, American author and journalist (*And the Band Played On*)

- Dinah Shore, American actress and singer

- Jule Styne, Anglo-American lyricist and composer ("It's Been a Long, Long Time")

- Barry Sullivan, American actor

- Jessica Tandy, English actress

- Bill Travers, English actor (*Born Free*) and animal rights activist

- Charles ("Bud") Wilkinson, American football player, coach and broadcaster

- Mai Zetterling, Swedish actress and film director

Spotlight on World Anniversaries

Leonardo da Vinci Death Anniversary

MAY 2, 1519 * 500 YEARS

Leonardo—legendary Renaissance painter, sculptor and inventor, the illegitimate son of an Italian notary—was born at Vinci, Republic of Florence, on Apr 15, 1452. He apprenticed in the workshop of Italian master Verrochio. His reputation as a universal genius began with 16th-century art historian Giorgio Vasari and continues today. Famous for the now iconic portrait of a silk merchant's wife, the *Mona Lisa*, for the often-reproduced mural of *The Last Supper* and for the drawing of the *Vitruvian Man*, he nevertheless produced few finished paintings—currently some 15 authenticated works exist—perhaps related to his reputation for perfectionism, procrastination, unsuccessful experimental painting techniques and interests so wide-ranging they were manifested in an inability to focus.

Museum exhibits worldwide are commemorating the artist's 500th death anniversary. At the Museo Leonardiano, in Tuscany, Italy, visitors can see an exhibition linking Leonardo's work to the landscape of his birth, including his earliest surviving drawing (1473), often regarded as Europe's first landscape drawing. Buckingham Palace in London, England, will show 200 Leonardo drawings from the British Royal Collection of more than 500 and The Queen's Gallery in Edinburgh, Scotland, will feature 80 of the drawings, following a nationwide exhibit of 12 different drawings in 12 UK cities. In the Netherlands, the Teylers Museum will feature drawings from European collections focusing on Leonardo's physiognomic studies. Florence's Uffizi Gallery will host *Codex Leicester, Water as a Microscope of Nature*, featuring perhaps Leonardo's most famous notebook, while the Museo Galileo will host *Leonardo and His Books*.

In France, a major exhibit at the Louvre in Paris will include the *Mona Lisa* and the museum's four other Leonardo works, as well as *Salvator Mundi* from the Louvre Abu Dhabi, while at Amboise, France, where he died, an exhibit will feature Leonardo's tapestry (1533) of *The Last Supper*, made for Francis I and lent by the Vatican Museums.

An increasing scholarly and public focus on Leonardo's 30 notebooks, including the Codex Leicester, which Bill Gates purchased in 1994 for some $30 million, has manifested itself recently in commercially mounted traveling exhibitions that have appeared from Bogotá to Budapest and include interactive exhibits and large-scale models of his inventions, machines and facsimiles of the notebooks.

Whether imagining fantastical flight machines, managing a painting studio, designing elaborate pageants and theatricals or painting sublime religious works, the sum of Leonardo's disparate interests has contributed to his reputation as the quintessential Renaissance man.

For information:

Leonardo da Vinci: A Life in Drawing
May 24–Oct 13
The Queen's Gallery
Buckingham Palace
London, England
Web: www.royalcollection.org.uk/visit/the-queens-gallery-buckingham-palace

Leonardo da Vinci: A Life in Drawing
Nov 22, 2019–Mar 15, 2020
The Queen's Gallery
Palace of Holyroodhouse
Edinburgh, Scotland
Web: www.royalcollection.org.uk/visit/the-queens-gallery-palace-of-holyroodhouse

Leonardo da Vinci: A Life in Drawing
Feb 1–May 6
Twelve simultaneous UK locations:

Ulster Museum
Belfast, Northern Ireland
Web: www.nmni.com/whats-on/leonardo-da-vinci

Birmingham Museum and Art Gallery
Birmingham, England
Web: www.birminghammuseums.org.uk/bmag

Bristol Museum & Art Gallery
Bristol, England
Web: www.bristolmuseums.org.uk/bristol-museum-and-art-gallery

National Museum Cardiff
Cathays Park, Cardiff, Wales
Web: https://museum.wales/cardiff/

Kelvingrove Museum
Glasgow, Scotland
Web: www.glasgowlife.org.uk/
museums

Leeds Art Gallery
Leeds, England
Web: www.leeds.gov.uk/
museumsandgalleries/
leedsartgallery/
visitor-information

Walker Art Gallery
Liverpool, England
Web: www.liverpoolmuseums.org.
uk/walker/

Manchester Art Gallery
Manchester, England
Web: www.manchesterartgallery.
org/exhibitions-and-events/

Millennium Gallery
Sheffield, England
Web: www.museums-sheffield.org.
uk/

Southampton City Art Gallery
Southampton, England
Web: www.
southamptoncityartgallery.com

Sunderland Museum and Winter
Gardens
Sunderland, England
Web: www.seeitdoitsunderland.
co.uk/about

A further location to be
announced.

**Drawings from European
collections focusing on da Vinci's
physiognomic studies**
Oct 5, 2018–Jan 6, 2019
Teylers Museum
Haarlem, The Netherlands
Web: www.teylersmuseum.nl/en

**Codex Leicester, Water as a
Microscope of Nature**
Oct 29, 2018–Jan 20, 2019
The Uffizi Gallery
Florence, Italy
Web: www.uffizi.com

Leonardo and His Books
April
Museo Galileo
Florence, Italy
Web: www.museogalileo.it/en

**Exhibition linking da Vinci's work
to the landscape of his birth**
April–June
Museo Leonardiano
Vinci, Tuscany, Italy
Web: www.museoleonardiano.it/eng

**Exhibition of the *Mona Lisa* and
four other Leonardos, plus *Salvator
Mundi* from Louvre Abu Dhabi**
Autumn
Louvre Museum
Paris, France
Web: www.louvre.fr/en

**Exhibition around the tapestry
(1533) of *The Last Supper***
June 1–Sept 2
Clos Lucé, da Vinci's last home
Amboise, France
Web: www.vinci-closluce.com/en

Birth Anniversary of Queen Victoria

MAY 24, 1819 * 200 YEARS

Born May 24, 1819, at Kensington
Palace, London, Queen Victo-
ria of Great Britain and Ireland,
Empress of India, was one of the
British Empire's most influen-
tial monarchs. Daughter of King
George III's fourth son, Prince
Edward, and Princess Victoria of
Saxe-Coburg-Saalfeld, she was the
last ruler of the house of Hanover,
as her son and successor, King
Edward VII, was of the house of
Saxe-Coburg-Gotha.

Immediately enamored with her
first cousin Prince Albert of Saxe-
Coburg-Gotha, Victoria proposed
marriage five days after their introduction. Albert, named Prince

Consort, had a lasting impact in
both public and personal arenas,
helping shape Victoria's views on
political and social matters, notably
that the monarchy should, publicly,
be above political party. They had
nine children who married into
Europe's royal families; upon her
death, Victoria had 42 grandchil-
dren and 37 great-grandchildren,
earning her the nickname the
"Grandmother of Europe." Notable
heirs include eldest grandson, Kaiser
Wilhelm II of Germany, and granddaughter Alexandra, the last tsarina
of Russia. Upon Albert's death in
1861, Victoria remained in lifelong
mourning, although she relied heavily on the advice and companion-
ship of her personal servant John
Brown, rumored to be her lover.

Victoria's ascension to throne on
June 20, 1837, marked a period of
scientific, industrial, political, cultural and military change so significant it is called the Victorian Age.
Widely known for its strict cultural
norms, the era dictated standards
of personal morality, virtue, propri-
ety, hard work, thrift, honesty and
devotion to duty exemplified by its
leader, who declared at age 11: "I will
be good." During Victoria's reign,
burgeoning middle-class prosper-
ity was both the result and cause of
the empire's transition to an indus-
trialized nation. Political changes
included the acquisition of the Suez
Canal (1875) and consolidation of
Great Britain's role as a world power;
its reach expanded to its greatest
extent, covering one-quarter of the
earth's land (4 million square miles)
and 124 million people. Meanwhile,
voting system reform during this
era lessened the influence of the
monarchy and House of Lords while
increasing power of the House of
Commons, resulting in the establishment of the constitutional monarchy.

Britain's longest-serving monarch until great-great-granddaughter Elizabeth II, Victoria was beloved and restored dignity and popularity to a besmirched crown while reigning during its transition from a political to a ceremonial power. Henry James wrote, "We all feel a bit motherless today" after her death Jan 22, 1901, at Osborne House, Isle of Wight. The extensive reach of her popularity and legacy remain evident in the many eponymous places, awards and commemorations celebrating her around the globe, including Victoria Falls, the Victorian Medal, and Canada's Victoria Day.

Birth Anniversary of Mohandas Karamchand Gandhi

OCT 2, 1869 * 150 YEARS

Born at Porbandar, India, Gandhi studied law in London, England, but difficulties in finding work in India led him to South Africa in 1893, where he experienced its extreme discrimination and racism toward nonwhites. Influenced by the Hindu Jain tradition of nonviolence, he formulated what would become the bedrock of civil disobedience: *satyagraha* ("truth and firmness"), often translated as "passive resistance," around which he organized protests of unfair

poll taxes and the government's refusal to recognize Hindu marriages. Gandhi returned to India in 1915, adopting the simple lifestyle and penitential fasting he used to highlight injustice or compel action from his followers or the British government.

Increasingly known as "Mahatma" (Great Soul), he led the Indian National Congress and spearheaded India's home rule movement through nonviolent protests and massive noncooperation efforts that included boycotting British taxes, goods and civil institutions. Most famously, from Mar 12 to Apr 6, 1930, he protested an increased salt tax by walking 240 miles in his trademark homespun white shawl, dhoti and sandals to the Arabian Sea and illegally making his own salt. Thousands joined him, and the British arrested over 60,000 people, including Gandhi. Nevertheless, the British were still forced to reduce the tax. Advocating economic independence and social reforms to improve the lives of women and untouchables, Gandhi also promoted unity between Hindus and Muslims and was nominated five times for a Nobel Peace Prize. Assassinated by a radical Hindu on Jan 30, 1948, Gandhi left a legacy that inspired civil rights leaders Martin Luther King, Jr, Nelson Mandela and Myanmar's Aung San Suu Kyi.

In 2014, to prepare for Gandhi's 150th birth anniversary, the Indian government launched a cleanliness program and has built millions of toilets to address the millions of people without plumbing. The Ministry of Culture has formed an international committee to plan celebratory events between October 2019 and October 2020. The Navajivan Trust is organizing a global

World Salt Day (World Sabras Day), arts expositions, time capsules and numerous educational events. In the United States, the Mahatma Gandhi Library is coordinating events that include plays, concerts, book clubs and festivals, including "1000 Lights for Peace," and the US Gandhian Society has launched a campaign, Gandhi Going Global, to promote Gandhi's legacy.

For information:

Gandhi 150
The Navajivan Trust

Behind Vidyapeeth, Ashram Rd
Ahmedabad, Gujarat 380014
E-mail: contact@gandhi150.in
Web: www.gandhi150.in/
   gandhi-vision

Ministry of Culture
Government of India
E-mail: office-hcm@gov.in
Web: www.indiaculture.nic.
   in/150th-birth-anniversary-
   mahatma-gandhi-committee

Mahatma Gandhi Sesquicentennial
Mahatma Gandhi Library

4526 Bermuda Dr
Sugarland, TX 77479
E-mail: info@gandhilibrary.org
Web: http://gandhi150.us/

Gandhi Going Global
Gandhian Society US

1412 Oak Tree Rd
Iselin, NJ 08830
E-mail: contact@gandhiansociety.
   org
Web: http://gandiansociety.org

Bauhaus

1919 * 100 YEARS

Founded in Weimar, Germany, in 1919 by architect Walter Gropius, the Bauhaus embodied a then-radical concept for an art school:

creating a curriculum unifying pursuit of the "fine arts"—painting and sculpture—with the "decorative arts"—furniture, textile, ceramic and metalwork design—by creating a new guild of craftsmen creating useful, beautiful objects using a collective, interdisciplinary approach. Study of materials, color theory and formal relationships preceded study in craft workshops. The Bauhaus aesthetic stressed function and utility and focused on simplified geometric forms in designing everything from lighting fixtures to tableware, wallpaper, furniture and stained glass. In 1923, financial practicalities obliged Gropius to reposition the original craftsmanship focus by stressing design for mass production. The curriculum also evolved to include photography and typography and, after eight years, architecture.

Gropius's utopian vision lasted 14 years, including successive leadership under architects Hannes Meyer and Ludwig Mies van der Rohe and relocations to Dessau in 1925 and then to Berlin, where it closed under Nazi pressure in 1933. Worldwide influence of the Bauhaus continues today, no doubt assisted by the immigration of key figures to the United States during World War II, and the people associated with it are synonymous with 20th-century modernism: Paul Klee, Vasily Kandinsky, Josef Albers, Lázló Moholy-Nagy, Marcel Breuer, Anni Albers and Marianne Brandt, among others.

Events across Germany will mark the centenary, including exhibitions at the Dessau Bauhaus Foundation, the opening of a new Bauhaus Museum in Weimar and a series of events in Berlin kicked off by a weeklong festival. Started in 2018, "Bauhaus Imaginista," a series of shows exploring the interaction between the Bauhaus and non-European modernist movements staged in Japan, China, Russia and Brazil with satellite events, workshops and panels in the United States, India, Morocco and Nigeria, culminates in 2019 at Berlin's Haus der Kulturen der Welt.

For information:

Bauhaus Dessau Foundation

Dessau, Germany
Web: www.bauhaus-dessau.de/
foundation.html

Weimar Bauhaus Foundation

Weimar, Germany
Web: www.klassik-stiftung.de/en/
institutions/museums

Bauhaus-Archiv/Museum für Gestaltung

Berlin, Germany
Web: www.bauhaus.de/en/

"Bauhaus Imaginista"

An international exhibition in four chapters

Chapter 1: *Correspondence*
Aug 4–Oct 8, 2018
The National Museum of Modern Art
Kyoto, Japan
Web: www.momak.go.jp/English/

Chapter II: *Designing Life*
Apr 8–July 8, 2018
The China Design Museum
Hangzhou, China
Web: www.design-china.
org/post/90168580519/
china-design-museum
and
Garage Museum of Contemporary Art
Moscow, Russia
Sept 11–Nov 30, 2018
Web: www.garagemca.org/ru

Chapter III: *Learning From*
Oct 10, 2018–Jan 10, 2019

The SESC Pompéia
São Paulo, Brazil
Web: www.sescsp.org.br

Chapter IV: *Undead*
Mar 15–June 10, 2019
The Haus der Kulturen der Welt
Berlin, Germany
Web: www.hkw.de/de/index.php

The Bauhaus Centenary

Visit Berlin
E-mail: hallo@visitBerlin.de
Web: www.visitberlin.de/en/
events-100-years-bauhaus

Siege of Leningrad Ends

JAN 27, 1944 * 75 YEARS

The Soviet city of Leningrad was a major target during World War II because German leader Adolf Hitler saw the city as a symbol of Lenin (whom he hated) and Bolshevism and recognized the tactical significance of its shipyards and munitions manufacturing. Pinned between the Finnish army to the north and the German army to the south, Leningrad, with a population of over three million, was effectively blockaded after Germans began shelling the city on Sept 4, 1941, finally severing communication and supply routes on Sept 8.

The city was shelled continually during the 872 days of the siege, its meager food stores burned before a bitterly cold winter came early in 1941. Faced with no power, no water supply and little food, the population of Leningrad starved and froze, burning furniture and floorboards and tried to survive on bread rations adulterated with cellulose and cottonseed—an estimated 300 calories per day. Desperate citizens eventually ate boiled leather, sawdust, wallpaper paste and some even resorted to cannibalism. An unstable, perilous "Road of Life" was created across the frozen Lake Ladoga each winter to bring military equipment and insufficient food to the starving city and to evacuate citizens. A precarious railway corridor was established in early 1943, but the siege lasted until the Red Army drove the Nazis west of the city in early 1944. The final civilian death toll has been estimated at more than one million.

The city (which reverted to its original name of Saint Petersburg in 1991) was awarded the Order of Lenin in 1945 and named a Hero City in 1965 and remains a symbol of Soviet tenacity.

D-Day

JUNE 6, 1944 * 75 YEARS

At dawn on June 6, 1944, 159,000 Allied troops landed on the beaches of German-occupied Normandy on the northern coast of France, marking "the beginning of the end" of World War II. Codenamed "Operation Overlord," the major offensive organized by General Dwight Eisenhower of the United States opened a second front in Europe to prevent Germany from invading Britain, 20 miles to the west, and from defeating Russian forces to the east.

The prior evening, widespread airborne deception operations by Britain's RAF drew Germany's attention to other locations. Before dawn, some 24,000 Allied troops parachuted inland to Normandy to take out bridges and seize the beaches' exit points while military gliders flew in additional equipment and weapons. At daybreak, 135,000 soldiers

from Britain, Canada and the United States braved brutal German resistance and choppy seas in the English Channel to storm five beaches across 50 miles west of France's Orne River. The British and Canadians overcame light opposition to capture Gold, Juno and Sword beaches, as did the Americans at Utah beach. At Omaha beach, 2,000 American lives were lost in the bloody siege before troops started to reach the seawall and drive back German forces.

Despite heavy losses, the Allies conquered all five beaches by nightfall, and the five D-Day beaches were unified on June 11. More than 4,000 Allied troops lost their lives in the D-Day invasion, with more than 10,000 wounded or missing. Many are laid to rest in the Normandy American Cemetery overlooking Omaha beach, the first American cemetery on European soil in World War II. Germany suffered similar casualties. The bloody amphibious battle, today known as D-Day, gave the Allies a foothold in France and kicked off the liberation of Western Europe from Nazi Germany. The Allied invasion repelled German forces while Soviet forces moved in from the east, leading to Germany's ultimate surrender the following May.

An international 75th anniversary commemoration will be held in France during the two-week Normandy D-Day Festival, a freedom celebration of peace concerts, liberation celebrations, a nautical rally, parachute jumps and historical reenactments. Additional commemorations will take place at the National World War II Memorial on the National Mall in Washington, DC, and the National D-Day Memorial in Bedford,

VA. Normandy's five "Plages du Débarquement" have been proposed as a UNESCO World Heritage site, to be considered at the World Heritage Committee's July 2019 meeting.

For information:

Normandy D-Day Festival 2019

Office de Tourisme de Bayeux Intercom
Claire Beauruel, Communication and Press Manager

4 place Gauquelin Despallières
14400 Bayeux, France
Phone: 33 (0) 2 31 51 28 24
E-mail: cbeauruel@bayeux-tourism.com
Web: www.ddayfestival.com.

National World War II Memorial

National Park Service
Mike Litterst, Public Affairs Specialist

900 Ohio Dr SW
Washington, DC 20024
Phone: (202) 245-4676
E-mail: Mike_Litterst@nps.gov
Web: www.nps.gov/nwwm

National D-Day Memorial

Angela Hatcher Lynch, Associate Director of Marketing
3 Overlord Circle
Bedford, VA 24523
Phone: (540) 586-3329
E-mail: alynch@dday.org
Web: www.dday.org

Apollo 11 Moon Landing

JULY 20, 1969 * 50 YEARS

At the height of the Cold War, the Apollo space program provided the free world with a powerful symbolic win, demonstrating the strength of the United States in technological and economic advancement. On July 20, 1969,

Spotlight on World Anniversaries

astronaut Neil Armstrong became the first human to set foot on the moon, declaring the historical moment "one small step for [a] man, one giant leap for mankind."

Eight years previous, the Soviet Union had shamed the United States by launching the first man into space, and President John F. Kennedy challenged Congress to achieve the goal "of landing a man on the moon and returning him safely to Earth" by the end of the 1960s. The subsequent space race united American political parties and brought together 400,000 scientists, technicians, tradesmen and engineers in a common goal of beating the Soviets to put a man on the moon.

On July 16, 1969, the *Apollo* 11 spacecraft launched from Florida's Kennedy Space Center carrying mission commander Armstrong, lunar module pilot Buzz Aldrin and command module pilot Michael Collins. Four days later, Collins orbited the moon in the command module *Columbia* while Armstrong and Aldrin alit the *Eagle* lunar module on the surface. Upon touchdown, Armstrong radioed to Mission Control Center in Houston that "the *Eagle* has landed." At 10:39 p.m. ET, Armstrong descended the ladder to the moon's surface as the world watched; Aldrin soon followed. An unprecedented 600 million people around the globe, 14 percent of the planet's total population, watched the moon landing on live television, a world record that's remarkable considering it occurred in the middle of the night in Europe and was blacked out in most of the Eastern Bloc.

Upon their return, Armstrong, Aldrin and Collins rode in tickertape parades in New York, Chicago and Los Angeles and were bestowed the Presidential Medals of Freedom. A 37-day "Giant Leap" tour through 23 countries followed, with visits with world leaders, including Queen Elizabeth II and Pope Paul VI. To this date, the United States remains the only country to have landed humans on a celestial body other than Earth and safely returned them home. *Apollo* technological spinoffs include memory foam, water filters and antiglare glass.

For the *Apollo*'s 50th anniversary, the command module *Columbia*, the only portion of the spacecraft that returned to Earth, has left the Smithsonian's National Air and Space Museum for the first time in 46 years as part of the traveling exhibition "Destination Moon: The Apollo 11 Mission," at the Senator John Heinz History Center in Pittsburgh, PA, through Feb 18, 2019, then Seattle's Museum of Flight Mar 16–Sept 2, 2019. In time for 2019, the Historic Apollo Mission Control Center at NASA's Johnson Space Center in Houston, TX—a National Historic Landmark—is being fully restored to its 1969 state with the authentic consoles used to monitor nine Gemini, all Apollo moon and 21 space shuttle missions. The US Mint will mark the anniversary with a series of commemorative coins, proceeds from which will be paid to the Smithsonian's "Destination Moon" exhibit, the Astronauts Memorial Foundation and the Astronaut Scholarship Foundation.

For information:

Space Center Houston

Meridyth Moore, Public Relations Specialist

1601 NASA Parkway
Houston, TX 77058
Phone: (281) 244-2139
E-mail: MMoore@spacecenter.org
Web: https://spacecenter.org

NASA

Bob Jacobs, Deputy Associate Administrator for Communications
NASA Headquarters

300 E St SW, Ste 5R30
Washington, DC 20546
Phone: (202) 358-1600
E-mail: bob.jacobs@nasa.gov
Web: www.nasa.gov

Johnson Space Center

JSC Newsroom
Phone: (281) 483-5111
E-mail: jsccommu@mail.nasa.gov
Web: www.nasa.gov/centers/johnson

"Destination Moon"

Smithsonian Institution
Jennifer Schommer, Assistant Director of PR

PO Box 37012, MRC 941
Washington, DC 20013-7012
Phone: (202) 633-3121
E-mail: schommerj@si.edu
Web: www.sites.si.edu/s/topic/0TO36000000L5O6GAK/destination-moon-the-apollo-11-mission

United States Mint

Office of Corporate Communications
Phone: (202) 354-7222
E-mail: Apollo11@usmint.treas.gov
www.usmint.gov/news/apollo-11

Spotlight on American Anniversaries

Birth Anniversary of Walt Whitman

MAY 31, 1819 * 200 YEARS

Premier 19th-century American poet Walt Whitman was born May 31, 1819, at West Hills, NY. Although renowned for his poetry, Whitman's career spanned many industries, including work as a journalist and editor, as a clerk for both the US Department of the Interior and the US Attorney General's office and as a Civil War hospital nurse in Washington, DC, the seldom-sterile hospital exposed him to viruses and diseases that are suspected of ruining his health. His personal life remains the subject of intense scrutiny and speculation because of his close relationships with other men, notably Peter Doyle, and the inferred homoeroticism in his poetry.

Whitman is most well known for his book of poetry *Leaves of Grass*, which he revised, expanded and reorganized for republication nine times during his life. It grew from 12 poems in its initial anonymous publication (1855) to 383 poems in the "deathbed" edition

(1891–1892). In it, Whitman was the first to experiment with the unrhymed, unmetered form of free verse. Of the 1855 edition, literary icon Ralph Waldo Emerson wrote it was a "wonderful gift . . . the most extraordinary piece of wit and wisdom that America has yet to offer," although it was otherwise widely derided. To the praise, Whitman responded, "I was simmering, simmering, simmering; Emerson brought me to a boil."

In *Leaves* and other works, Whitman incorporated native idiom, vibrant American rhythm and a variety of poetic expression, which reflected his view of poetry as the distillation of experience. Whitman's work provided a frank presentation of subject matter, notably the body and sensuality, the latter of which caused no small amount of consternation among his critics, who declared it indecent.

Paralyzed on the left side following a stroke in 1873, Whitman continued to work on his seminal text until his death Mar 26, 1892, at Camden, NJ. Underappreciated during his life, Whitman is now widely regarded as the great poet of democracy; his work bridged the Transcendentalist and Realist literary eras and influenced many 20th-century American poets. Bicentennial commemorations include the Walt Whitman Bicentennial May 31–June 2, 2019,

in Plainview, NY, and the Walt Whitman International Festival at Walt Whitman Birthplace, Huntington Station, NY, Aug 9–11, 2019.

For information:

Walt Whitman Birthplace State Historic Site

246 Old Walt Whitman Rd
South Huntington, NY 11746-4148
Phone: (631) 427-5240
Web: www.waltwhitman.org

Alabama's Bicentennial

DEC 14, 1819 * 200 YEARS

Established in 1817 as the Alabama Territory, Alabama became a state in 1819, and 2019 marks its 200th statehood anniversary. Geographical and topographical features, including the East Gulf Coastal Plain and part of the Appalachians, make the Yellowhammer State among the country's most biologically and geologically diverse states. US Census data estimates 2018 population at 4,863,300. Ranking second nationally for fish, poultry and peanut production in 2015, it is first in pulp and third in paper production. The top five industries are automotive (nearly one million vehicles produced in

2017), chemical, technology, forestry and aeronautics.

Widely viewed culturally as the buckle of the Bible Belt and dominated in numbers by Baptists, it is also home to the Eternal Word Television Network, the world's largest religious media network, founded by a Catholic nun. Native Harper Lee wrote, arguably, the novel most often assigned in American classrooms, *To Kill a Mockingbird*, while native Helen Keller gained worldwide acclaim as an author and activist. Born-in-Alabama musicians Hank Williams, Sr, Nat "King" Cole, Lionel Richie and Emmylou Harris have made seminal contributions in their genres. In sports, Alabama can claim boxing champion Joe Louis, track legend Jesse Owens, baseball stars Willie Mays and Hank Aaron, and Paul "Bear" Bryant, widely regarded as the 20th century's greatest college football coach. Alabama is home to nine historically black colleges and universities, including Stillman College and Tuskegee University.

Bicentennial celebrations have already begun—kicking off in Mobile, the state's oldest city (founded 1702)—and span three years, concluding Dec 14, 2019, in Montgomery, the capitol. The Alabama Bicentennial Commission has a constantly updated calendar of events (www.alabama200.org/participate/events/events-calendar).
For information:

ALABAMA BICENTENNIAL COMMISSION

PO Box 246 Montgomery, AL 36103 Phone: (334) 242-4537 Bicentennial commission e-mail: Debra.Pascal@bicentennial.alabama.gov
Media contact e-mail: media@alabama200.org
Web: www.alabama200.org

MAKING ALABAMA: A BICENTENNIAL TRAVELING EXHIBIT

Four identical exhibits will travel to all 67 Alabama counties between March 2018 and November 2019. For a listing of current exhibit locales, see the website at: www.makingalabama.org/hosting-exhibit.

Birth Anniversary of Jackie Robinson

JAN 31, 1919 * 100 YEARS

Revered for breaking the color barrier in sports when he joined the Brooklyn Dodgers in 1947, Jack Roosevelt Robinson was born Jan 31, 1919, at Cairo, GA, the grandson of a slave. Robinson's groundbreaking integration of professional baseball

paved the way for racial integration in all professional sports. Throughout his baseball career, Robinson was an outspoken advocate of civil rights. Dr. Martin Luther King, Jr, later said Robinson helped jumpstart the civil rights movement, stating he was "a pilgrim that walked in the lonesome byways toward the high road of Freedom. He was a sit-inner before sit-ins, a freedom rider before freedom rides."

Robinson's quest for racial equality neither started nor ended during his tenure in professional baseball. He and heavyweight champion Joe Louis protested to end unequal treatment of servicemen of color while stationed at Fort Riley, KS, during WWII, resulting in the desegregation of officer training. A believer in black capitalism, after retiring from baseball in 1957, Robinson worked as vice president for Chock Full O'Nuts, a restaurant chain that employed many black workers; was integral in founding Harlem's African-American owned and controlled Freedom National Bank, serving as its chairman of the board; and created the Jackie Robinson Construction Company, which built housing for black families. He played an active role in Harlem's YMCA and raised money for the NAACP's Freedom Fund and black churches destroyed by hate groups. Robinson stood alongside Dr. King at 1963's March on Washington and spoke and marched with King in Birmingham, AL.

Named Rookie of the Year in 1947 and MVP in 1949, Robinson was inducted into the Baseball Hall of Fame in 1962 before his death Oct 24, 1972, at Stamford, CT. On Apr 15, the anniversary of his major league debut, MLB celebrates Jackie Robinson Day in commemoration of his historic achievements both on and off the field. Players wear jerseys with 42, Robinson's number, which was retired league-wide in 1997.

Chicago Race Riots of 1919 and the "Red Summer"

SUMMER 1919 * 100 YEARS

The riots of 1919 were the bloody flashpoint of a convergence of post-WWI social ills caused by the rapid demobilization of 2.6 million men and the ensuing job and housing shortages combined with inflation, unemployment, black migration northward and a white fear of Bolshevik revolutionary infiltration into nascent African-American civil rights activities. Summer 1919 had already seen smaller riots in Charleston, SC; Longview, TX; and Washington, DC, when on July 27, 17-year-old Eugene Williams crossed an unofficial, invisible segregation barrier on a Chicago South Side beach. Williams drowned after being stoned by white men. The police refused to arrest the men involved, sparking violence that spread quickly, in part, because unlike other cities that rioted, Chicago's rioters were organized by members of territorial "athletic clubs," politically connected clubs of young white men that fomented long-standing racial tensions on the city's South Side and who had been waiting to instigate or take part in a riot. The violence met organized resistance from an angered black population, many of them veterans who expected greater civil freedoms after their service. By Aug 1, 23 black and 15 white men had died, hundreds were injured and more than 1,000 black families had lost their homes to fires.

By October 1919, 21 more cities would experience riots, including New York, Omaha and Elaine, AR, where on Sept 30, black sharecroppers were organizing a union, supporting rumors that pro-Communist insurgents were inciting revolutionary activities. During the confrontation, a white man was killed, and a wave of reprisals descended on eastern Arkansas, leaving more than 200 African Americans dead. The country also suffered a marked increase in lynchings, with 52 taking place during these months.

In the aftermath, the National Association for the Advancement of Colored People (NAACP) gained thousands of new members, overturned convictions of black defendants unfairly prosecuted after the riots and raised public awareness about continued lynchings, which subsequently declined in number. The response of African Americans to the Red Summer, both in their resistance to violence and their continued push for equal rights, laid the groundwork for the later civil rights movement of the 1960s.

World Series "Black Sox" Scandal

OCT 1–9, 1919 * 100 YEARS

"Say It Ain't So, Joe," the plaintive *Chicago Daily News* headline, captured the general public's initial response to news that eight Chicago White Sox players had confessed to a Grand Jury their involvement in fixing the 1919 World Series by throwing it in favor of the Cincinnati Reds.

The heavily favored White Sox handed Cincinnati a first-ever World Series win in the best-of-nine games playoff, winning three games to the Reds' five. Although subsequently cleared of the charges following their 1921 indictment hearing, when all paper records of their confessions mysteriously disappeared, the players were dubbed the "Black Sox" for their part in the scandal, which had stood to net them $100,000 for throwing the series. All the players—first baseman C. Arnold "Chick" Gandil, pitchers Eddie Cicotte and Claude "Lefty" Williams, shortstop Charles "Swede" Risberg, outfielder Oscar "Happy" Felsch, third baseman Buck Weaver, utility infielder Fred McMullin and power hitter "Shoeless" Joe Jackson—were banned for life from playing organized baseball by Kenesaw Mountain Landis, who had recently been appointed as baseball's first commissioner.

Infamous New York gambler/racketeer Arnold Rothstein is often mentioned as a major player in the bribery scheme, although his involvement has never been proven. Most probably, numerous gamblers were involved, including Joseph "Sport" Sullivan, "Sleepy" Bill Burns, Bill Maharg and Abe Attell. And the tightfistedness of White Sox owner Charles Comiskey contributed to player discontent. Maharg went public with his knowledge of the fix, precipitating the confessions of Cicotte, Jackson, Williams and Felsch.

Their professional baseball careers ruined, several spent time playing semipro ball or for outlaw teams, but each eventually ended up working outside baseball, with varying degrees of success, often at a series of jobs, which included tavern and pool-hall owner, house painter, truck driver, game warden, factory lineman, crane operator and restaurateur. Continued public interest and controversy around the players' punishment has found expression in literature and film, including F. Scott Fitzgerald's character Meyer Wolfsheim in *The Great Gatsby*, said to be based on Rothstein; Bernard Malamud's 1952 novel *The Natural* and its 1984 film adaptation; Dan Gutman's 2002 novel *Shoeless Joe & Me*; W.P. Kinsella's 1982 novel *Shoeless Joe*, adapted into the 1989 film *Field of Dreams*; and director John Sayles's 1988 film *Eight Men Out*, a dramatization of Eliot Asinof's well-known 1963 history of the scandal *Eight Men Out: The Black Sox and the 1919 World Series*.

The Stonewall Uprising

JUNE 28, 1969 * 50 YEARS

A routine police raid on a New York City gay bar in the summer of 1969 escalated into a spontaneous uprising credited as the birth of the modern LGBTQ civil rights movement.

At 3 AM on Saturday, June 28, police raided the Stonewall Inn—a gathering place for disenfranchised queer youth, drag queens, gay men and lesbians—for selling liquor without a license. The Public Morals Squad roughed up patrons and, per New York criminal statute, arrested anyone not wearing gender-appropriate clothing. When hit in the head with a nightstick, a handcuffed woman yelled to witnesses, "Why don't you do something?" inciting bystanders on Christopher Street to fight back. Police barricaded themselves in the club, but rioters threw flaming trash through the broken windows, chanting "Gay power!" and "We want freedom!" Reinforcements extinguished the fire and dispersed the crowd, but the riot made the daily newspapers, and thousands of demonstrators returned to the West

Village over the next several nights in a unique display of civil disobedience and street theater, where gay cheerleaders defied fire hoses and police batons with bawdy taunts, chants of "fag power" and campy renditions of "We Shall Overcome."

While there had been gay rights demonstrations before, Stonewall was the flash point that inspired the oppressed to fight for LGBTQ rights. On the first anniversary of the uprising, the first gay pride marches in the United States took place in New York, Chicago and Los Angeles. On the second anniversary, marches sprang up in Boston, Dallas, Milwaukee, London, Paris, West Berlin and Stockholm. Today, most gay pride festivities around the world take place at the end of June to mark the Stonewall uprising. Christopher Street and environs were designated a National Historic Landmark in 1999, as was the Stonewall Inn in 2000. In 2016, President Barack Obama designated the Stonewall Inn, the street in front of it and the park across the street the Stonewall National Monument, making it the country's first national monument designated for an LGBT historic site. In 2019, the epic WorldPride celebration will be held in the United States for the first time, in New York City, to mark the 50th anniversary of the

Stonewall Riots. Themed "Millions of Moments of Pride," Stonewall 50/WorldPride 2019 will offer two months of events and programs along with NYC Pride's historic march, rally and PrideFest in June.

For information:

STONEWALL 50

Eboni Munn, Communications
  Manager

NYC Pride
154 Christopher St, Ste 1D
New York, NY 10012
Phone: (212) 807-6424
E-mail: eboni@nycpride.org
Web: www.stonewall50.org

STONEWALL NATIONAL MONUMENT

Minerva Anderson, Chief of
  Communications, National Parks
  of New York Harbor
Federal Hall National Monument
  c/o Stonewall National
  Monument

26 Wall St New York, NY 10005
Phone: (212) 825-2208
E-mail: Minerva_Anderson@nps.
  gov
Web: www.nps.gov/ston/index.htm

STONEWALL INN

Kurt Kelly, Owner

53 Christopher St
New York, NY 10014
Phone: (212) 488-2705
E-mail: KKelly@
  thestonewallinnnyc.com
Web: thestonewallinnnyc.com

Woodstock Music and Art Fair

AUG 15–18, 1969 * 50 YEARS

The Woodstock Music and Art Fair is a watershed event that nourished the fertile ground at the intersection of pop and rock music with youth, community and the burgeoning American counterculture. But in August 1969, it sounded like a disaster waiting to happen. Promoter infighting, shaky funding and area venues' reticence to admit thousands of "hippies" forced it onto the improvised site of Max Yasgur's farm at Bethel, Sullivan County, New York. With logistics lacking, Woodstock, originally ticketed, became entirely free to the hundreds of thousands of fans who swarmed the area. When it finally went off, over 30 acts performed from Thursday, Aug 15, through the early morning of Monday, Aug 18, when Jimi Hendrix delivered his frenzied, unforgettable electric guitar rendition of the "Star-Spangled Banner."

Hendrix, The Grateful Dead, Richie Havens, The Who, Janis Joplin, Joan Baez, Sly & the Family Stone, Creedence Clearwater Revival, The Band and Crosby, Stills, Nash & Young all delivered iconic sets at Woodstock. But its stunted promotion and organizational drift prompted heavyweights like Bob Dylan, Joni Mitchell and Led Zeppelin to turn down offers to play. For many artists in 1969, Woodstock sounded like just another fest, and one being held on a pig farm to boot.

Today, Yasgur's farm is the site of the nonprofit Bethel Woods Center for the Arts (BWCA), which includes a performance amphitheater and a Woodstock museum. With grants from New York State and other benefactors, BWCA hosts an event series slated to run from 2017 through 2019, Woodstock's 50th anniversary year, designed to promote the music, message and memories of that muddy August weekend.

For information:

BETHEL WOODS CENTER FOR THE ARTS

PO Box 222
Liberty, NY 12754
Phone: (866) 781-2922
E-mail: info@bethelwoodscenter.org
Web: www.bethelwoodscenter.org

Spotlight on People

The year 2019 brings many significant birth anniversaries, of which the following is a selection. See "Spotlight on World Anniversaries" and "Spotlight on American Anniversaries" for longer profiles of Leonardo da Vinci, Queen Victoria, Walt Whitman, Mohandas Gandhi and Jackie Robinson. See also the main book for many other significant birth anniversaries.

World History

Niccolò Machiavelli

Birth * May 3, 1469 * 550 years

Writer, statesman and political philosopher, Machiavelli, like other intellectuals and artists of the Renaissance, looked to classical antiquity to inform his subject—contemporary politics—and worked within the patronage system common in his day. His personal, political and intellectual relationship with his patrons, the powerful Florentine Medici family, informed his writing and career, especially *The Prince*, his most famous work (published in 1532), which prescribes strong, absolute government. The tenor of his advice inspired the adjective "Machiavellian," meaning cunning, scheming and unscrupulous in political or career advancement. Born at Florence, Republic of Florence, Machiavelli died there June 21, 1527.

Catherine de' Medici

Birth * Apr 13, 1519 * 500 years

Born in Florence, Republic of Florence, Catherine, the daughter of Lorenzo de' Medici, married King Henry II of France. After his death, she became more powerful through her influence over her three sons who would successively reign as king: Francis II (1559–1560), Charles IX (1560–1574) and Henry III (1574–1589). She attempted to secure the power of the monarchy and the unity of France by alternately favoring the Catholic aristocracy and French Huguenots (Protestants), but lacking religious feeling herself, she was short-sighted about the hatred of each faction toward the other, and France was submerged in the Wars of Religion between 1562 and 1598. A collector of books and paintings, she built churches and palaces, including Tuileries, Monceaux and Chenonceaux. She died at Blois, France, Jan 5, 1589.

Arthur Wellesley, Duke of Wellington

Birth * May 1, 1769 * 250 years

British general and statesman, born in Dublin, Ireland. Wellesley, after success as a military tactician in India, entered the Napoleonic fray in 1808, becoming a national hero for his leadership in the Peninsular Wars that drove the French out of Spain and led to Napoleon's abdication (1814). After returning to France in 1815, decisively defeating Napoleon in a brilliant victory at the Battle of Waterloo, he became the Duke of Wellington. He then served as commander-in-chief, prime minister (1828–1830, 1834) and leader of the House of Lords. Autocratic, blunt, conservative and opposed to reform, he earned the moniker "The Iron Duke," and was impervious to public opinion: "Trust nothing to the enthusiasm of the people. . . . Give them a strong, and just, and if possible, a good government." He died Sept 14, 1852, at Walmer Castle, Kent, England.

Napoleon Bonaparte

Birth * Aug 15, 1769 * 250 years

French emperor, military genius, founder of the Legion of Honor, born in Ajaccio, Corsica. A general at age 24, Napoleon emerged as a leader as the French Revolution ran out of steam. Named emperor in 1804, his empire ranged from the Atlantic to the Russian border. His difficulties enforcing a naval blockade of British goods led him to a war in both Spain and, disastrously, Russia, where his army was forced into a winter retreat that killed all but 40,000 of 500,000 men. After abdicating in 1815, he returned from exile only to be roundly defeated at the Battle of Waterloo. A reformer, Napoleon created a centralized government, a national police force and the foundation for the French legal system, the Napoleonic Code, which he called "the sheet anchor which will save France, and it will entitle me to the benedictions of posterity." Bonaparte died in exile on the island of St. Helena, May 5, 1821.

Prince Albert of Saxe-Coburg-Gotha

Birth * Aug 26, 1819 * 200 years

Born at Rosenau, Germany, Albert is known for his marriage to England's Queen Victoria (1840). Though an arranged marriage, it was one of love and devotion, with Albert serving as Victoria's confidant, chief advisor and personal secretary; he was made Prince Consort in 1857. Her confinement during the births of their nine children necessitated his more active, visible involvement in running the empire and family. At his urging, Victoria transformed the monarchy to a politically neutral constitutional monarchy, and the royal family became a moral force that exemplified Victorian ideals. An accomplished musician, Albert was also keenly interested in the era's rapid scientific and technological advances. After his death of typhoid fever Dec 14, 1861, at Windsor Castle, Victoria proclaimed, "My life as a happy one is ended! The world is gone for me!"

Louis Riel

Birth * Oct 22, 1844 * 175 years

Born at the Red River Colony (near what is now Winnipeg, MB, Canada), Louis Riel, leader of the Metis (French/Indian mixed ancestry), was elected to Canada's House of Commons in 1873 and 1874 but was never seated. Having been confined to asylums for madness (feigned or falsely charged, some said), Riel became a US citizen in 1883. In 1885, he returned to western Canada to lead the North West Rebellion. Defeated, he surrendered and was tried for treason, convicted and hanged at Regina, Canada, on Nov 16, 1885. Seen as a patriot and protector of French culture in Canada, Riel became a legend and a symbol of the problems between French and English Canadians.

Neville Chamberlain

Birth * Mar 18, 1869 * 150 years

Career politician born Arthur Neville Chamberlain at Edgbaston, Birmingham, England. He is (in)famously associated with the appeasement of Adolf Hitler while British prime minister from 1937 to 1940. Following election in 1911 to the Birmingham city council and service as lord mayor from 1915 to 1916, he was elected in 1918 to Parliament. Subsequently, he held positions as postmaster general, paymaster general, minister of health and chancellor of the exchequer. As prime minister, determined to avert war, he successfully counseled accepting the Munich Agreement of 1938, but after Hitler invaded Poland in September 1939, his government declared war. Dissatisfaction with his handling of the war led to his resignation on May 10, 1940. He died Nov 9, 1940, at Heckfield, near Reading, Hampshire.

Nikita Khrushchev

Birth * Apr 15, 1894 * 125 years

Born in Kalinovka, Russia, Khrushchev led the Communist Party after Joseph Stalin's death in 1953 and became premier in 1957, ushering in a period of reform marked by the release of political prisoners, less censorship and increased contact with the West. His Cold War stance of "peaceful coexistence" was tested by shooting down an American spy plane in 1960 and the Cuban Missile Crisis in 1962. Backing down from the crisis was an embarrassment for the USSR, and his signing the Nuclear Test Ban Treaty in 1963 strained Soviet relations with Maoist China, and Khrushchev was removed from power in 1964. Nonetheless, his legacy of opening Communism to the idea of reform has endured. He died Sept 11, 1971, at Moscow, Russia.

Rudolf Hess

Birth * Apr 26, 1894 * 125 years

One of the most bizarre figures of WWII Germany, Walter Richard Rudolf Hess was born at Alexandria, Egypt. He was a close friend, confidant and personal secretary to Adolf Hitler, who had dictated much of *Mein Kampf* to Hess while both were prisoners at Landsberg Prison. Third in command in Nazi Germany, Hess surprised the world on May 10, 1941, by flying alone to Scotland and parachuting from his plane on what he called a "mission of humanity": offering peace to Britain if it would join Germany in attacking the Soviet Union. He was immediately taken prisoner of war. At the Nuremberg Trials (1946), after questions about his sanity, he was convicted and sentenced to life imprisonment at Spandau Allied War Crimes Prison at Berlin, Germany. Outliving all other prisoners there, he was the only inmate from 1955 until he succeeded (in his fourth attempt) in committing suicide. He died at West Berlin, Germany, Aug 17, 1987.

Edward VIII

Birth * June 23, 1894 * 125 years

Edward Albert Christian George Andrew Patrick David, King Edward VIII, was born at Richmond Park, England, and became Prince of Wales in July 1911. He ascended to the English throne upon the death of his father, George V, on Jan 20, 1936, but the coronation never took place. He abdicated on Dec 11, 1936, in order to marry "the woman I love," twice-divorced American Wallis Warfield Simpson. They were married in France on June 3, 1937. Edward was named Duke of Windsor by his brother successor, George VI. The duke died at Paris, France, May 28, 1972, but was buried in England, near Windsor Castle.

Esther Afua Ocloo

Birth * Apr 18, 1919 * 100 years

Ghanaian pioneer of microlending and cofounder of Women's World

Banking, "Auntie Ocloo" sought to improve women's economic opportunities. She famously said, "Women must know that the strongest power in the world is economic power." She started Nkulenu Industries while in secondary school; within six years, it was Ghana's premier food-processing plant. The first black graduate of London's Good Housekeeping Institute, Ocloo shared the Africa Prize for Leadership in 1990. Using half of her $100,000 award, she established a program to teach women agricultural, food preservation, textile and leatherwork skills. Born Esther Afua Nkulenu in British Togoland (now Ghana), she died at Accra, Ghana, Feb 8, 2002.

Eva Perón

Birth * May 7, 1919 * 100 years

The youngest of five children in a working-class family, Perón was born María Eva Duarte at Los Toldos, Argentina. She made a name for herself in theater before marrying Juan Perón and taking on the role for which she is best known, Argentina's first lady. Her advocacy of women's suffrage, labor rights and social welfare programs endeared her to *los descamisados* ("the shirtless ones") and incited opposition from the *gente bien*

("social elite"). During her tenure as first lady, women gained the right to vote (1947), many new hospitals were built and infection rates of communicable disease fell dramatically under her unofficial supervision of the Departments of Labor and Health. Her untimely death from cancer on July 26, 1952, at Buenos Aires thrust the nation into profound grief, and her funeral—attended by an estimated three million people—was befitting a head of state.

Sir Edmund Percival Hillary

Birth * July 20, 1919 * 100 years

Explorer, mountaineer, born at Tuakau, near Auckland, New Zealand. With Tenzing Norgay, a Sherpa guide, Hillary became first to ascend the summit of the highest mountain in the world, Mount Everest (29,035 feet), at 11:30 a.m., May 29, 1953. "We climbed because nobody climbed it before," he said. Hillary continued mountaineering and exploration, including trekking around the Antarctic continent in 1957–58. He also flew to the North Pole in 1985 (with Neil Armstrong), thus becoming the first human to have stood at the Everest summit and on both poles. He established the Sir Edmund Hillary Himalayan Trust and led many conservation and humanitarian efforts. Hillary, who also listed his occupation as beekeeper, died Jan 11, 2008, at Auckland. The daunting 40-foot sheer rock face near the summit of Everest was christened the Hillary Step in his honor—the 2015 Nepal earthquake changed its features.

Pierre Elliott Trudeau

Birth * Oct 18, 1919 * 100 years

The youthful, charismatic and "with it" Trudeau caused a sensation when he became the prime minister of Canada in 1968. In fact, the sensation was called "Trudeaumania," and it rivaled reactions to The Beatles earlier in the 1960s. The yoga- and judo-practicing Trudeau (or "PET," as he went by) promised change and new ideas while at the same time dating glamorous women and hobnobbing with John Lennon and Yoko Ono. Trudeau was prime minister from 1968 to 1979 and 1980 to 1984—taken together, the terms equate to 15 ½ years of service, the third longest by a Canadian prime minister. Born at Montreal, QC, Canada, he died there Sept 28, 2000. His son, Justin, is currently Canadian prime minister—the first time a relative of a former office holder has been elected to that position.

Mohammad Reza Pahlavi, Shah of Iran

Birth * Oct 26, 1919 * 100 years

Born in Tehran, Persia (now Iran), Reza became shah in 1941. A dictator, he nationalized the oil industry and led a series of reforms known as the White Revolution that included greater freedoms for women and politically expedient land reforms that consolidated his power. Claims that his reforms were anti-Islamic and that the shah himself was overly reliant on Western support gained increasing traction among a disenfranchised populace. Increasingly violent demonstrations forced him into exile in 1979, and Iran became an Islamic republic. When he was admitted to the United States for medical treatment, Iranian militants seized 52 Americans as hostages to force the shah's extradition. The United States refused, and the hostages spent 444 days in captivity before their release in 1981. The shah died in exile at Cairo, Egypt, July 27, 1980.

American History

Elbridge Gerry

Birth * July 17, 1744 * 275 years

Lifelong American statesman, his name became part of the language ("gerrymander") after he signed a redistricting bill favoring his party while governor of Massachusetts in 1812. Son of a wealthy merchant and a graduate of Harvard University, Gerry served during his life in numerous capacities, including the Massachusetts Provincial Congress, special envoy to France under President John Adams, two-time representative to the Continental Congress and fifth vice president of the United States (1813–1814) during the James Madison administration. Born at Marblehead, MA, Gerry died at Washington, DC, Nov 23, 1814.

Abigail Adams

Birth * Nov 22, 1744 * 275 years

Wife of John Adams and mother of John Quincy Adams, second and sixth presidents of the United States, Abigail Adams is one of only two women with this distinction in American history. An intelligent woman interested in politics and current affairs, Adams was a prodigious letter writer, an influence on her husband and the successful caretaker of her household and family finances. An early proponent of women's rights, she argued to her husband as the new

From the Gettysburg Oration by Edward Everett

We have assembled, friends, fellow citizens . . . to pay the last tribute of respect to the brave men who, in the hard-fought battles of the first, second, and third days of July last, laid down their lives for the country on these hillsides and the plains before us, and whose remains have been gathered into the cemetery which we consecrate this day. As my eye ranges over the fields whose sods were so lately moistened by the blood of gallant and loyal men, I feel, as never before, how truly it was said of old that it is sweet and becoming to die for one's country. I feel, as never before, how justly, from the dawn of history to the present time, men have paid the homage of their gratitude and admiration to the memory of those who nobly sacrifice their lives, that their fellow-men may live in safety and in honor. And if this tribute were ever due, to whom could it be more justly paid than to those whose last resting-place we this day commend to the blessing of Heaven and of men?

American government took form that Congress "would remember the ladies. . . . Do not put such unlimited power into the hands of the husbands. Remember, all men would be tyrants if they could. If particular care and attention is not paid to the ladies, we are determined to foment a rebellion, and will not hold ourselves bound by any laws in which we have no voice or representation." Born at Weymouth, MA, she died Oct 28, 1818, at Quincy, MA.

Edward Everett

Birth * Apr 11, 1794 * 225 years

American statesman, scholar and orator, born at Dorcester, MA. Everett was US secretary of state under President Millard Fillmore. He also served as governor of Massachusetts, as well as US senator and representative from that state. Famed as an orator, it was Everett who delivered the main address at the dedication of Gettysburg National Cemetery on Nov 19, 1863—an address of more than two hours. President Abraham

Lincoln also spoke at the dedication, and his brief speech (less than two minutes) has been called one of the most eloquent in the English language. Once a candidate for vice president of the United States (1860), Everett died at Boston, MA, Jan 15, 1865.

Julia Ward Howe

Birth * May 27, 1819 * 200 years

American author, feminist, social activist and orator Julia Ward Howe was born at New York, NY. Famous for "Battle Hymn of the Republic," composed after visiting

military camps during the Civil War (1862), Howe was a prolific author and, with husband Samuel Gridley Howe, edited the antislavery paper *The Commonwealth*. Her social activism extended beyond the abolition movement to the women's suffrage and peace movements. Howe was president of the American branch of the Women's International Peace Association and organized the New England Women's and American Women's Suffrage Associations; the latter focused solely on women's suffrage rather than advocating for broader social justice issues like the more progressive Anthony-Stanton National Women's Suffrage Association. The first woman elected to the American Academy of Arts and Letters (1908), Howe died Oct 17, 1910, at Newport, RI.

Allan Pinkerton

Birth * Aug 25, 1819 * 200 years

Born in Glasgow, Scotland, Pinkerton founded a national detective agency at Chicago, IL, in 1850. Before the FBI existed, Pinkerton's agency (still in existence) provided criminal investigation, crime prevention and intelligence services on a national scale, and he ran a spy network for the Union army during the Civil War. A friend of fellow abolitionist John Brown, he also operated a stop on the Underground Railroad in Dundee, IL. Hired by the railroad, coal and steel companies to infiltrate unions and police labor disputes, his agency later became synonymous with strikebreaking and violent anti-union activities. He died at Chicago, July 1, 1884.

Mary Mallon (Typhoid Mary)

Birth * Sept 23, 1869 * 150 years

Known as "Typhoid Mary," Mallon's career as a cook resulted in lasting infamy. Born at Cookstown, Ireland, Mallon immigrated to the United States as a teenager. Little is known about her life in New York City before epidemiologist George A. Soper took interest in her as a suspected carrier of typhoid during an outbreak investigation in that city. Mallon was confined to Riverside Hospital upon testing positive but promised to change her vocation to obtain her release. She instead assumed an alias and resumed her former occupation, eventually working at Sloane Hospital for Women. A typhoid outbreak soon followed in 1915, resulting in a second arrest on Mar 27, 1915, and confinement at Riverside Hospital on North Brother Island until her death Nov 11, 1938, at New York, NY.

George Wallace

Birth * Aug 25, 1919 * 100 years

Four-time Democratic governor of Alabama (1962, 1970, 1974, 1982) who campaigned three times for president, Wallace is considered widely influential in the "southernization" of American politics

for his early and consistent insistence on the overweening power of judges, oppressive bureaucrats and the threat the federal government posed to ordinary people's freedoms. A longtime champion of states' rights, he gained national attention as a symbol of segregation when he defied federal mandates to desegregate schools by blocking enrollment of black students at the University of Alabama in 1963. Shot while campaigning for the Democratic presidential nomination in 1972, Wallace was permanently paralyzed below the waist. Born at Clio, AL, he died Sept 13, 1998, at Montgomery, AL.

Religion and Philosophy

Báb, born Sayyed `Alí Muhammad

Birth * Oct 20, 1819 * 200 years

Born at Shiraz, Qajar Iran, Sayyed `Alí Muhammad, descendant of the Prophet Muhammad, declared he was "Al-Báb" (the gateway) to the imam on May 23, 1844, in the *Qayyūm al-asmā'*, a commentary on the Qur'ān, which proclaimed a new prophet would overturn old customs and usher in a new era. Soon thereafter, he and 18 disciples, the sacred Bābī number 19, disseminated his message of Bábism throughout Persia. Suspected of fomenting insurrection and found guilty of heresy by religious judges, he was executed July 9, 1850, at Tabriz. One of his earliest disciples, Bahā Allāh, later proclaimed himself the messenger prophesized by the Báb; he founded the Bahā'ī faith on Bábism and declared the Báb one of its central prophets.

Friedrich Wilhelm Nietzsche

Birth * Oct 15, 1844 * 175 years

Influential, controversial and often misunderstood philosopher born at Röcken, Prussia, Nietzsche is especially remembered for his declaration that "God is dead." Contemporary scientific enlightenment, notably Darwinian theory, was a pivotal underpinning of Nietzsche's work. His "superman," self-assured and free from guilt, directly contradicted dominant Judeo-Christian morality. Major works include *Thus Spake Zarathustra*, *Beyond Good and Evil*, and *The Genealogy of Morals*—all attacked conventional morality. Nietzsche died at Weimar, Germany, Aug 25, 1900, a decade after suffering a mental breakdown.

Literature

Herman Melville

Birth * Aug 1, 1819 * 200 years

Novelist and poet, born at New York, NY, Melville enlisted as a seaman on a whaling ship in 1841. Deserting his post, he lived with natives on the Marquesas Islands, was imprisoned as a deserter in Tahiti and eventually joined the US Navy, returning home in 1844. He found early literary success with *Typee* (1846) and *Omoo* (1847), both adventures set in the South Seas. When his magnum opus, *Moby-Dick* (1851), and later works went largely unread, Melville turned to poetry and found steady work as a customs officer, dying unlauded at New York City, Sept 28, 1891. Only in the 1920s was *Moby-Dick* finally recognized as one of the great American novels and Melville's genius finally recognized.

George Eliot

Birth * Nov 22, 1819 * 200 years

Victorian English novelist George Eliot, whose real name was Mary Ann Evans, was born at Nuneaton, Warwickshire, England. Eliot's career began as a translator, notably of Ludwig Feuerbach's *Essence of Christianity*, before she began writing for and editing *The Westminster Review*. Her novels, including *Silas Marner*, *Adam Bede*, and *Middlemarch*, employed realism and grappled with humanistic versus religious morality. Eliot's scandalous relationship with George Henry Lewes initially shocked Victorian society; however, their London home soon became an intellectual and literary mecca. She died at Chelsea, London, England, Dec 22, 1880.

André Gide

Birth * Nov 22, 1869 * 150 years

French writer, intellectual and critic, born in Paris, France. Gide wrote voluminously and confessionally in autobiographical works and novels such as in *The Counterfeiters* (1927) to define his credo that self-discovery required brutal honesty and a willingness to jettison traditional morality. His travels to North Africa awakened him to his homosexuality, for which he wrote a defense in *Corydon* (1924), and later works attacked French colonial abuses of power and the failings of Communism. France's preeminent man of letters in the first half of the 20th century, he won the Nobel Prize for Literature in 1947. Gide died Feb 19, 1951, at Paris, France.

Dashiell Hammett

Birth * May 27, 1894 * 125 years

The man who brought realism to the genre of mystery writing, Samuel Dashiell Hammett was born at St. Mary's County, MD. His first two novels, *Red Harvest* (1929) and *The Dain Curse* (1929), were based on his eight years spent as a Pinkerton detective. Hammett is recognized as the founder of the "hard-boiled" school of detective fiction. Many of his novels have been made into films: *The Maltese Falcon* (1930), considered by many to be his finest work; *The Thin Man* (1932), which provided the basis for a series of five movies starring William Powell and Myrna Loy; and *The Glass Key* (1931). Hammett was called to testify but refused to name members of an alleged subversive organization during House Un-American Activities Committee hearings. Plagued by years of illness and the effects of alcoholism, he died Jan 10, 1961, at New York City, cared for by his longtime partner, playwright Lillian Hellman.

Aldous Huxley

Birth * July 26, 1894 * 125 years

English author, satirist, mystic and philosopher, Huxley was born at Godalming, Surrey, England, into a family of intellectual prominence. Educated at Eton and at Oxford, where he read English literature and philosophy, he graduated in 1915. His novel *Point Counter Point* (1928) was an international success, but he is probably best known for *Brave New World* (1932), dramatizing the dehumanizing control of humans through social conditioning, drugs and economic necessity. In "Vulgarity in Literature" he wrote, "The fact that many people should be shocked by what he writes practically imposes it as a duty upon the writer to go on shocking them." Huxley died at Los Angeles, CA, Nov 22, 1963.

Spotlight on People

E.E. Cummings

Birth * Oct 14, 1894 * 125 years

Born Edward Estlin Cummings at Cambridge, MA. American avant-garde poet and painter, son of a prominent Unitarian minister and a mother who encouraged his writing from an early age. Cummings created a distinctive personal style characterized by nonstandard grammatical and linguistic usage and precise, spare language, typically arranging a few key words eccentrically on the page. This experimentation with poetic form and language ranks him among the most innovative poets of his time. A Harvard graduate, Cummings became a highly popular performer on the academic circuit in the 1950s. In all, he wrote 12 volumes of verse, assembled in his 2-volume *Complete Poems* (1968). He died Sept 3, 1962, at North Conway, NH.

James Grover Thurber

Birth * Dec 8, 1894 * 125 years

Author, playwright, cartoonist and editor at *The New Yorker* magazine. His short story "Is Sex Necessary?" (1929), coauthored with E.B. White, satirized popular contemporary psychosexual literature and illustrated early one of his recurrent themes. His autobiography, *My Life and Hard Times* (1933), established Thurber among humorists of the first rank. Taken together, his 1939 story "The Secret Life of Walter Mitty" and its film adaptations (1947 and 2013); the Broadway productions of *The Male Animal* (1940)—cowritten with Elliott Nugent—and *A Thurber Carnival* (1960), along with his bestselling *The Years with Ross* (1959), cemented his reputation as one of America's foremost humorous authors. Born at Columbus, OH, Thurber died Nov 2, 1961, at New York City.

Jerome David (J.D.) Salinger

Birth * Jan 1, 1919 * 100 years

Reclusive author, born at New York City. Following military service in WWII as a counterintelligence officer, he published seven stories in *The New Yorker* that garnered wide critical and popular attention and established him among the leading short story writers of the period. In 1951, he published *The Catcher in the Rye*, a bestselling novel widely considered a classic of American literature and famous for its portrayal of adolescent protagonist Holden Caulfield. Later works included *Franny and Zooey* (1961), *Raise High the Roof Beam, Carpenters* and *Seymour: An Introduction* (1963) and *Hapworth 16, 1924* (1965). Married three times and a father of two, Salinger died at Cornish, NH, Jan 27, 2010.

Doris Lessing

Birth * Oct 22, 1919 * 100 years

Born at Kermanshah, Persia, British author Doris Lessing created a body of work known for its feminism, as well as its explorations of the complex themes of racism in colonial Africa, women's roles in male-dominated spheres, politics and interpersonal relationships. Hailed as "one of the most honest, intelligent, and engaged writers of the day" (*New York Times Book Review*, Lesley Hazelton, 1982), she was awarded the Nobel Prize for Literature in 2007. Major works include *The Golden Notebook* and the Children of Violence series. She died Nov 17, 2013, at London, England.

Children's Literature
Richard McClure Scarry

Birth * June 5, 1919 * 100 years

Author and illustrator of children's books, Scarry was born at Boston, MA. Two widely known books of the more than 250 authored by Scarry are *Richard Scarry's Best Word Book Ever* (1965) and *Richard Scarry's Please & Thank You* (1973). The pages are crowded with small animal characters who live like humans. More than 100 million copies of his books have been sold worldwide. Scarry died Apr 30, 1994, at Gstaad, Switzerland.

Journalism
Anne Royall

Birth * June 11, 1769 * 250 years

America's first woman journalist was born Anne Newport in New Baltimore, MD. After her husband William's death left her penniless at age 54, Royall traveled across the United States, writing her observations to support herself; those 10 publications remain a valuable source of American social history. Her acerbic observations won her many enemies: in 1829, she was successfully prosecuted as a "common scold"—quarrelsome nuisance—for her unrelenting criticism of a Washington, DC, Presbyterian church; her fine was paid by John Eaton, Andrew Jackson's secretary of war. Unable to continue her travels, she became a Washington, DC–based reporter and editor who exposed the abuses of government first in *Paul Pry* (1831–1836; a newspaper typeset by orphans) and then in *The Huntress* (1836–1854). Royall died at Washington, DC, Oct 1, 1854.

Ben Hecht

Birth * Feb 28, 1894 * 125 years

In the course of his career, Ben Hecht wrote in many genres. His newspaper column, "1,001 Afternoons in Chicago," popularized human-interest sketches. His play *The Front Page*, written with Charles MacArthur, was a hit on Broadway (1928) and on film (1931). He was a successful reporter, and his first novel, *Eric Dorn*, resulted partly from his time reporting from Berlin after WWI. Hecht wrote or cowrote a number of successful movie scripts, including *Notorious* and *Wuthering Heights*. Born at New York City, he died there Apr 18, 1964.

Malcolm Forbes

Birth * Aug 19, 1919 * 100 years

Publisher, born at New York, NY. Malcolm Forbes was an unabashed proponent of capitalism, and his beliefs led to his colorful and successful climb to the top of the magazine-publishing industry. Known as much for his lavish lifestyle as his publishing acumen, Forbes was also an avid motorcyclist and hot-air balloonist. He died Feb 24, 1990, at Far Hills, NJ.

Jim Murray

Birth * Dec 29, 1919 * 100 years

James Patrick Murray, Jr, was born at Hartford, CT. After a peripatetic career writing for several newspapers and magazines, Murray settled in as sports columnist for the *Los Angeles Times*. Despite serious eye problems, family tragedy and a decided lack of ego, he excelled at his craft, becoming one of only four sportswriters to win a Pulitzer Prize for general commentary. He was given the J.G. Taylor Spink Award in 1987. Murray died at Los Angeles, CA, Aug 16, 1998.

Art, Architecture and Design

John Ruskin

Birth * Feb 8, 1819 * 200 years

Born in London, England, Ruskin was the son of wealthy evangelical Protestants who exposed him early to Continental travel and encouraged his artistic and literary tendencies. Ruskin attended Oxford University and later became England's first official professor of art there. Ruskin was a prolific and influential theorist and writer on art and architecture during the 19th century, a leader in the Gothic Revival movement, a champion of painter J.M.W. Turner and included the Pre-Raphaelites among his set. His works include *Modern Painters, The Seven Lamps of Architecture* and *The Stones of Venice*. In addition to his aesthetic interests, Ruskin was a social reformer and environmentalist. He died Jan 20, 1900, at Brantwood, England.

Jean Désiré Gustave Courbet

Birth * June 10, 1819 * 200 years

Realist painter, born in Ornans, France. Courbet's early paintings, such as *After Dinner at Ornans* (1849) and *Burial at Ornans* (1859), drew on the rural life of his native Franche-Comté without the veneer of Romanticism. Both his form of using larger-than-life canvasses for humble subjects and his technique of thickly applied paint disturbed conventional expectations and put him at the vanguard of Realist painters. His later landscapes, particularly *The Stormy Sea* (1869), would influence both Impressionist and Modernist artists. A Republican, he joined the antiroyalist Paris Commune in 1871 and was arrested for encouraging the toppling of the Vendôme column dedicated to Napoleon. Exiled to Switzerland, he died there at La Tour de Peilz Dec 31, 1877.

Mary Cassatt

Birth * May 22, 1844 * 175 years

Leading American artist of the Impressionist school, Mary Cassatt was born May 22, 1844, at Allegheny City, PA (now part of Pittsburgh). She settled in Paris, France, in 1874, where she was influenced by Degas and the Impressionists. She was later instrumental in their works becoming well known in the United States. The majority of her paintings and pastels were based on the theme of mother and child. After 1900, her eyesight began to fail, and by 1914 she was no longer able to paint. Cassatt died at Chateau de Beaufresne near Paris, June 14, 1926.

Sir Edwin Lutyens

Birth * Mar 29, 1869 * 150 years

English architect known first for his country houses assimilating the traditional building forms, styles and materials of the Surrey countryside into designs that addressed the contemporary domestic needs of his upper-middle-class clients. Influenced by the English Arts and Crafts movement aesthetic,

his collaborations with the famous landscape gardener Gertrude Jekyll typified his careful integration of buildings with romantically conceived gardens. Later work included buildings in the Neo-Georgian and Neo-Classical styles, famous war memorials and advising on the planning of New Delhi, India, where he designed the Viceroy's House. Lutyens was married to Emily Bulwer-Lytton, granddaughter of novelist Edward Bulwer-Lytton, and the father of five children. Born at London, England, he died there Jan 1, 1944.

Henri Matisse

Birth * Dec 31, 1869 * 150 years

Painter and sculptor, born at Le Cateau-Cambrésis, France. Matisse was a leading figure in the Fauve movement, which suited his preoccupation with unmodulated color, line and simplified forms. His shocking nude pastoral *Joie de vivre* (1906) is an early Modernist masterpiece and was followed by other seminal works, including *Dance I* and *Music* (1909–1910). Influenced by the art, textiles and decorative motifs he discovered on his extensive travels, Matisse experimented continually with the relationship between color and form, decoration and subject in his paintings and, later, collages made from paper cutouts. He designed and decorated the stained-glass Chapelle du Rosaire in Vence, France. Matisse died at Nice, France, Nov 3, 1954.

Norman Rockwell

Birth * Feb 3, 1894 * 125 years

American artist and illustrator of wide range, best known and beloved by many for highly detailed, often warm and humorous *Saturday*

Evening Post covers throughout the 1940s, 50s, and 60s celebrating family life and small-town America. In the late 60s and 70s, his subject matter turned more topical in illustrations for *Look*, including the space program, international politics and social issues. Classically trained, Rockwell early on developed an exacting technique that, throughout his long career, he also deployed in advertisements, calendars and commercial art, as well as in portraits of presidents, celebrities and world leaders. Born at New York, NY, he died at Stockbridge, MA, Nov 8, 1978.

Comics

Harold Lincoln Gray

Birth * Jan 20, 1894 * 125 years

The creator of "Little Orphan Annie" was born at Kankakee, IL. The comic strip featuring the 12-year-old Annie; her dog, Sandy; and her mentor and guardian, Oliver "Daddy" Warbucks, began appearing in the *Chicago Tribune* in 1924. While controversial for its strong conservative views, the strip was highly popular for its stories demonstrating the values of perseverance, independence and courage. Gray created the strip for 44 years until his death May 9, 1968, at La Jolla, CA, at age 74.

Elzie Crisler Segar

Birth * Dec 8, 1894 * 125 years

Popeye creator Elzie Crisler Segar was born at Chester, IL. Originally

called "Thimble Theater," the comic strip that came to be known as "Popeye" had the unusual format of a one-act play in cartoon form. Centered on the Oyl family, especially daughter Olive, the strip introduced a new central character in 1929. A one-eyed sailor with bulging muscles, Popeye became the strip's star attraction almost immediately. Popeye made it to the silver screen in animated form and in 1980 became a movie, with Robin Williams playing the lead. Segar died Oct 13, 1938, at Santa Monica, CA.

Music

Jacques Offenbach

Birth * June 20, 1819 * 200 years

Composer, born Jacob Offenbach in Cologne, Germany. Originally a cellist in the Opéra Comique, he became a conductor in the Théâtre Français in 1849. Opening his own theater, the Bouffes-Parisiens, in 1855, he pioneered the French comic opera. His operettas include *Orphée aux enfers* (*Orpheus in the Underworld*, 1858), which gave the world the music for the can-can; *La belle Hélène* (*Fair Helen*, 1864) and a final unfinished grand opera, *The Tales of Hoffmann*, finished and produced after his death. Offenbach died at Paris, France, Oct 5, 1880.

Clara Schumann

Birth * Sept 13, 1819 * 200 years

Born Clara Josephine Wieck at Leipzig, Germany, Schumann was a child piano prodigy who made her first concert tour at the age of eleven. She was one of the preeminent pianist-interpreters of the Romantic Movement in music in a career that lasted 60 years. She played pieces by memory—now a standard practice among concert pianists. She married composer Robert Schumann in 1840, and the couple famously mentored the young Johannes Brahms. Fate brought much tragedy to her life: Robert Schumann battled mental illness and died in 1856, and four of her eight children died at a young age. Clara struggled with maintaining the household and continuing her touring. Schumann was a composer and respected musical educator as well. She died May 20, 1896, at Frankfurt, Germany.

Bessie Smith

Birth * Apr 15, 1894 * 125 years

The "Empress of the Blues," Bessie Smith, was born at Chattanooga, TN (one source says in 1892). She was assisted in her efforts to break into show business by Ma Rainey, the first great blues singer. Her first recording was made in February 1923. Her hits included "Downhearted Blues," "St. Louis Blues" and "Empty Bed Blues." Smith died of injuries she sustained in an automobile accident at Clarksdale, MS, Sept 26, 1937. "Downhearted Blues" was chosen by the Library of Congress for its National Recording Registry in 2002.

Kitty Wells

Birth * Aug 30, 1919 * 100 years

Born Muriel Ellen Deason at Nashville, TN, this country singer was a pioneer in the music industry. One of the first commercially successful women ever signed to a major label, she was about to quit music to raise her family when she scored a surprise hit with 1952's "It Wasn't God Who Made Honky Tonk Angels." That song, the first by a woman to hit number one on the country charts, launched a career ranked the sixth-most-successful in the history of *Billboard*'s country charts. She died at Madison, TN, July 16, 2012.

Art Blakey

Birth * Oct 11, 1919 * 100 years

Born at Pittsburgh, PA, Blakey switched from piano to drums while still in his youth and by the late 1930s was gigging with pianist, arranger and fellow Pittsburgh native Mary Lou Williams. The 1940s found Blakey behind the kit for Billy Eckstine's big band, and by 1949 he was recording as a leader for Blue Note. *The Jazz Messengers* (1956, Columbia), with pianist Horace Silver, established him alongside that moniker, and Blakey retained it for the rest of his career. The Messengers concentrated on hard bop and jazz traditionalism; with Blakey as its leader, the group was an incubator for numerous jazz luminaries, including Wayne Shorter, Lee Morgan and Wynton Marsalis. "This is the music of my culture good, bad or indifferent," Blakey said of his life's work. "No America—no jazz. It's the only culture America has brought forth." He died Oct 16, 1990, at New York, NY.

Entertainment

Jack Benny

Birth * Feb 14, 1894 * 125 years

American comedian born Benjamin Kubelsky, Jack Benny entered vaudeville at Waukegan, IL, at age 17, using the violin as a comic stage prop. His radio show, "The Jack Benny Program," first aired in 1932 and continued for 20 years with little change in format. The show successfully transitioned to television and aired from 1950 to 1965. One of his most well-known comic gimmicks was his purported stinginess: when confronted by a mugger who growled, "Your money or your life," Benny replied, "I'm thinking it over." The recipient of a Golden Globe and Emmy, Benny was born at Chicago, IL, and died Dec 26, 1974, at Los Angeles, CA.

Martha Graham

Birth * May 11, 1894 * 125 years

Martha Graham was born at Allegheny, PA, and became one of the giants of the modern dance movement in the United States. She began her dance career at the comparatively late age of 22 and joined the Greenwich Village Follies in 1923. Her new ideas began to surface in the late 1920s and 30s, and by the mid-1930s she was incorporating the rituals of the southwestern Native Americans in her work. She is credited with bringing a new psychological depth to modern dance by exploring primal emotions and ancient rituals in her work. She performed until the age of 75 and premiered in her 180th ballet, *The Maple Leaf Rag*, in the fall of 1990. She died Apr 1, 1991, at New York, NY.

Joseph von Sternberg

Birth * May 29, 1894 * 125 years

Following work as a film cutter, making army training films and jobs as technical assistant, scenarist, camera man and experimental film director, Austrian Joseph von Sternberg had a career breakthrough when he made the film *Underworld* (1927), a *Kammerspiel*-influenced gangster story. His most famous films are those made with muse Marlene Dietrich from *The Blue Angel* (1930) in Germany to six in Hollywood, including *Blonde Venus* (1932) and *The Devil Is a Woman* (1935). "A painter in light," von Sternberg's chiaroscuro effects elicit comparisons to Rembrandt, while the frank sexuality and worldly irony of his stories oppose the traditional formula plotting and stock happy endings typically associated with Hollywood films. Born at Vienna, Austria-Hungary, von Sternberg died Dec 22, 1969, at Los Angeles, CA.

Ross Bagdasarian, Sr

Birth * Jan 27, 1919 * 100 years

Was David Seville just the exasperated human keeper of Alvin & the Chipmunks' leash? Well, not exactly. In reality, Seville was, like the famous high-pitched singing rodent combo themselves, the creation of Rostom Sipan "Ross" Bagdasarian, an itinerant entertainer with a family of his own to feed who first hit on the tape manipulation gimmick with the 1958 one-off hit "Witch Doctor." The son of Armenian immigrants, Bagdasarian was born at Fresno, CA. He served in the air force in World War II and even appeared in Alfred Hitchcock's *Rear Window* before the Chipmunks gambit really took off. The novelty took on a life of its own, and Bagdasarian's son Ross Jr took the reins of the franchise after Ross Sr died from a heart attack Jan 16, 1972, at Beverly Hills, CA.

Nat "King" Cole

Birth * Mar 17, 1919 * 100 years

Nathaniel Adams Cole was born at Montgomery, AL, and began his musical career at an early age, playing the piano at age four. He was the first black entertainer to host a national television show.

His many songs include "The Christmas Song," "Nature Boy," "Mona Lisa," "Ramblin' Rose" and "Unforgettable." Although he was dogged by racial discrimination throughout his career, including the cancellation of his television show because opposition from Southern white viewers decreased advertising revenue, Cole was criticized by prominent black newspapers for not joining other black entertainers in the civil rights struggle. Cole contributed more than $50,000 to civil rights organizations in response to the criticism. Nat King Cole died Feb 15, 1965, at Santa Monica, CA.

Pete Seeger

Birth * May 3, 1919 * 100 years

Legendary American folk singer/songwriter and political activist born at New York City, NY, Seeger is credited with saving folk music—and his signature instrument, the five-string banjo—from obscurity. Notable works include "If I Had a Hammer" and "Where Have All the Flowers Gone." A social justice activist, he popularized "We Shall Overcome," which later became the civil rights movement's anthem. Blacklisted for decades for a McCarthy-era conviction of contempt of Congress (eventually overturned), Seeger was later awarded the National Medal of Arts (1994), inducted into the Rock and Roll Hall of Fame (1996) and received two Grammys before his death on Jan 27, 2014, at New York City.

Liberace

Birth * May 16, 1919 * 100 years

Wladziu Valentino Liberace was a concert pianist who began with a piano, a candelabra, a brother named George and a huge engaging smile, threw in extravagant clothes and jewels and became a Las Vegas headliner and the winner of two Emmy Awards, six gold albums and two stars on the Hollywood Walk of Fame. Liberace was born at West Allis, WI; he died Feb 4, 1987, at Palm Springs, CA. He once stated of his winking, mink-berobed persona, "[Liberace] is a combination of music and personality and a certain amount of shock value. It`s a fantasy."

Margot Fonteyn

Birth * May 18, 1919 * 100 years

Born Margaret Hookman at Reigate, Surrey, England, Dame Margot Fonteyn thrilled ballet audiences for 45 years with her musicality, superlative acting and a refinement of style coupled with physical beauty and emotional passion. She emerged from the Sadler's Wells company (later the Royal Ballet) during the 1930s and '40s as a solo artist dancing both the classical repertoire and works choreographed for her. Her dance partnership with Soviet defector Rudolph Nureyev in the 1960s, starting with *Giselle* when she was 42 and he 23, electrified audiences. She died Feb 21, 1991, at Panama City, Panama.

Slim Pickens

Birth * June 29, 1919 * 100 years

A lifelong entertainer, Slim Pickens was a teenaged rodeo clown before hitting Hollywood and appearing in his first feature, 1950's *Rocky Mountain*. Perennially a crusty sidekick, townie wiseacre or jovial cowhand, Pickens worked steadily in film and television for three decades. His memorable ride on a hydrogen bomb as the hat-waving B-52 pilot in Stanley Kubrick's *Dr. Strangelove* (1964) secured his place in Hollywood folklore. Born Louis Burton Lindley at Kingsburg, CA, Pickens died Dec 8, 1983, at Modesto, CA.

Science and Technology

Baron Georges Léopold Nicolas Frédéric Cuvier

Birth * Aug 23, 1769 * 250 years

Father of paleontology, born at Montbéliard, France. Cuvier created a system of comparative anatomy based on the observation of distinct characteristics through which he defined four main groups of classification: vertebrates, mollusks, radiates and articulates. He came to believe that the parts of an organism were so interdependent as to prevent modification and thus opposed early theories of evolution. His study of fossils and their relationship to the strata where they were found provided crucial evidence for the concept of extinction through his careful reassembly of complete skeletons, and he also theorized a series of catastrophic events that might cause a species to cease to exist. Cuvier died at Paris, France, May 13, 1832.

Alexander Von Humboldt

Birth * Sept 14, 1769 * 250 years

Born at Berlin, Prussia, Von Humboldt was a scientific Renaissance man, with expertise spanning meteorology, botany, geology, geography and oceanography. His explorations and extensive writings greatly expanded Western society's knowledge—his detailed recording of every observation is one of his greatest legacies—along with his influential holistic view of the sciences. During an expedition to South and Central America (1799–1804), Von Humboldt discovered a connection between the Orinoco and Amazon rivers and the eponymous Peru Current, theorized that Ecuadorian volcanoes indicated a flaw in the earth's crust and collected thousands of plant specimens. He also first noted the ability of humans to alter their immediate climate. He created the isothermal map. Von Humboldt said, "I have . . . endeavored to comprehend the phenomena of physical objects in their general connection, and to represent nature as on a great whole, moved and animated by internal forces." Von Humboldt died May 6, 1859, at Berlin—by which time he was an international celebrity. His name lives on in scores of named geological features and botanical names.

Alfred Kinsey

Birth * June 23, 1894 * 125 years

Born at Hoboken, NJ, Kinsey was a professor of zoology who moved into the study of human sexual behavior in the 1940s at Indiana University's Institute for Sex Research (later renamed after him). Kinsey published two controversial books based on his research: *Sexual Behavior in the Human Male* (1948)—which sold 500,000 copies—and *Sexual Behavior in the Human Female* (1953). Kinsey died Aug 25, 1956, at Bloomington, IN.

J. Presper Eckert, Jr

Birth * Apr 9, 1919 * 100 years

Coinventor with John W. Mauchly of ENIAC (Electronic Numerical Integrator and Computer), which was first demonstrated at the Moore School of Electrical Engineering at the University of Pennsylvania at Philadelphia, Feb 14, 1946 (generally considered the birth of the computer age). Originally designed to process artillery calculations for the army, ENIAC was also used in the Manhattan Project. Eckert and Mauchly formed the Electronic Control Company, which later became Unisys Corporation. Eckert was born at Philadelphia and died at Bryn Mawr, PA, June 3, 1995.

Economics, Business and Labor

Edmund Ruffin

Birth * Jan 5, 1794 * 225 years

Born at Prince George County, VA, Edmund Ruffin was an American agriculturist whose discoveries about crop rotation and fertilizer were influential in the early agrarian culture of the United States. He published the *Farmer's Register* from 1833 to 1842, a journal that promoted scientific agriculture. A noted politician, as well as a farmer, he was an early advocate of Southern secession whose views were widely circulated in pamphlets. As a member of the

Palmetto Guards of Charleston, he was given the honor of firing the first shot on Fort Sumter on Apr 12, 1861. According to legend, after the South's defeat, he became despondent and, wrapping himself in the Confederate flag, took his own life on June 18, 1865, at Amelia County, VA.

Christopher Latham Sholes

Birth * Feb 14, 1819 * 200 years

Born at Mooresburg, PA, Sholes was a printer by trade and an inventor by nature. His passion for inventing resulted in many significant printing industry advances, notably the typewriter, cocreated with Samuel W. Soulé and Carlos Glidden, and the QWERTY keyboard, whose letters he arranged to create the fewest jamming incidences. Funding difficulties resulted in typewriter patent rights being sold to Remington. Other inventions include page numbering machines (cocreated with Soulé) and a machine, in use until the advent of computers, that addressed newspapers. Sholes died Feb 17, 1890, at Milwaukee, WI, following a lengthy battle with tuberculosis.

Elias Howe

Birth * July 9, 1819 * 200 years

Born at Spencer, MA, Howe patented a sewing machine in 1846, notable for its double-thread stitch and the innovation of placing the eye of the needle near its point. After unsuccessfully trying to develop a market in England, he returned to the United States penniless and discovered others were producing machines that infringed on his patent. He sued successfully and thereafter earned royalties on every machine made, making him a wealthy man as a ready-to-wear garment industry developed around the use of his machine. Howe died on Oct 3, 1867, at Brooklyn, NY.

George Meany

Birth * Aug 16, 1894 * 125 years

The labor leader was born at New York, NY. A plumber by trade, he became president of the American Federation of Labor (AFL) in 1952, and when he merged the AFL with the Congress of Industrial Organizations (CIO), he became the leading labor spokesperson in the United States. In 1957, he expelled Jimmy Hoffa's Teamsters Union from the AFL-CIO, and he lost the United Auto Workers in 1967. His tenure as president lasted until 1979. He died Jan 10, 1980, at Washington, DC.

James M. Buchanan

Birth * Oct 3, 1919 * 100 years

Born at Murfreesboro, TN, Buchanan was awarded the Nobel Prize for Economic Science in 1986 for his analyses of economic and political decision-making. Buchanan earned his BS (1940) and MS in Tennessee (1941) before serving in the US Naval Reserve. He completed a PhD at the University of Chicago (1948), a center of conservative economists, and went on to help shape a generation of conservative political thought about deficits, taxes and the size of government, contending that the pursuit of self-interest by modern politicians often led to harmful public results. He was cofounder of the Center for Study of Public Choice and a senior fellow at the libertarian Cato Institute. Buchanan died Jan 9, 2013, in Blacksburg, VA.

Sports

Abner Doubleday

Birth * June 26, 1819 * 200 years

Abner Doubleday served in the US Army during the Mexican War and the Seminole War in Florida prior to his service in the American Civil War. His service found him at the battles of Second Bull Run, Antietam and Fredericksburg, and as a major general he commanded a division at Gettysburg. A commission set up by sporting goods manufacturer Albert Spalding to investigate the origins of baseball credited Doubleday with inventing the game in 1839. Subsequent research has debunked the commission's finding. Doubleday was born at Ballston Spa, NY, and died at Mendham, NJ, Jan 26, 1893.

Abraham Gilbert Mills

Birth * Mar 12, 1844 * 175 years

Baseball executive, born at New York, NY. Mills carried a bat and baseball with him during his service in the Civil War. He was president of the National League and, as chairman of the Mills Commission in 1905, helped to enshrine as

fact the fanciful story that Abner Doubleday had invented baseball in Cooperstown, NY, in 1839. Mills died at Falmouth, MA, Aug 26, 1929.

Kid Nichols

Birth * Sept 14, 1869 * 150 years

Charles Augustus ("Kid") Nichols, Baseball Hall of Fame pitcher, was born at Madison, WI. Nichols was one of the greatest pitchers of the 19th century. In the 1890s, he led the Boston National League team to five championships in nine seasons, winning 30 or more games seven years in a row. Inducted into the Hall of Fame in 1949, he died at Kansas City, MO, Apr 11, 1953.

John Heisman

Birth * Oct 23, 1869 * 150 years

John William Heisman, football player, coach and administrator, was born at Cleveland, OH. Heisman played football at Brown and Pennsylvania and began coaching at Oberlin. He moved to Akron, Oberlin again, Auburn, Clemson, Georgia Tech, Pennsylvania, Washington and Jefferson, and Rice. After his retirement, he became athletic director at the Downtown Athletic Club in New York. The club's award to the best college football player in the country was named in his honor posthumously. Heisman died at New York, NY, Oct 3, 1936.

Eddie Robinson

Birth * Feb 13, 1919 * 100 years

One of the winningest coaches in college football history, born at Jackson, LA. As the head coach at Grambling State University in Grambling, LA, he led the Tigers to more than 400 victories during his 56-year tenure (1941–1997). Considered a civil rights pioneer for his leadership in an era when doors were not always open for black athletes, he battled segregation and ultimately sent more than 200 players to the NFL. He was elected to the College Football Hall of Fame immediately upon his retirement in 1997 and was diagnosed with Alzheimer's that same year. He died at Ruston, LA, Apr 3, 2007.

Tom Harmon

Birth * Sept 28, 1919 * 100 years

Thomas D. Harmon, Heisman Trophy halfback and broadcaster, born at Rensselaer, IN. Harmon became a national figure by his exploits in the backfield for the University of Michigan. Known as "Old 98," his uniform number, he won many awards, including the Heisman in 1940. After service in World War II, during which he bailed out twice from destroyed planes, Harmon played two years with the Los Angeles Rams. After retiring, he worked as a sportscaster. Harmon died at Los Angeles, CA, Mar 15, 1990.

Miscellaneous

William Spooner

Birth * July 22, 1844 * 175 years

Reverend William Archibald Spooner was born at London, England, and was a warden of New College, Oxford, from 1903 to 1924. He was infamous for his frequent slips of the tongue that led to coinage of the term "spoonerism" to describe them. The accidental transpositions of this scholarly man gave us "blushing crow" (for crushing blow), "tons of soil" (for sons of toil), "queer old dean" (for dear old queen), "swell foop" (for fell swoop) and "half-warmed fish" (for half-formed wish). He died at Oxford, England, Aug 29, 1930.

Spotlight on 2019 Events

International Year of the Periodic Table of Chemical Elements

Jan 1–Dec 31, 2019

To coincide with the 150th anniversary of the discovery of the Periodic System by Russian scientist Dmitry Mendeleev, a father of modern chemistry, the United Nations has proclaimed 2019 as the International Year of the Periodic Table of Chemical Elements (IYPTCE). Mendeleev's defining 1869 breakthrough was the prediction of properties of five elements and their compounds; he also left space in the Periodic Table for elements to be discovered in the future. The Periodic Table, a unique tool enabling scientists to predict the appearance and properties of matter on Earth and in the universe, is an example of science's global language, with broad implications in astronomy, chemistry, physics, biology and other natural sciences.

Administered by UNESCO and the International Union of Pure and Applied Chemistry, IYPTCE is a recognition of the important role of the basic sciences, especially chemistry and physics, while also paying tribute to the recent discovery and naming of four super-heavy elements of the Periodic Table with atomic numbers 113 (Nihonium), 115 (Moscovium), 117 (Tennessine) and 118 (Oganesson) resulting from close international scientific cooperation. The opening ceremony kicks off the year Jan 29 at UNESCO Headquarters, Paris. A symposium, "The Periodic Table at 150" during IUPAC's centenary coincides with a celebration of the 150th anniversary of Mendeleev's Periodic Table during the 47th World Chemistry Congress in Paris in July. Additional commemorations will take place at the Mendeleev International Chemistry Olympiad (Paris, April); the Markovnikov Congress (June); the International Chemistry Olympiad (Paris, July); the EuCheMs Inorganic Chemistry Conference (Greece, June) and the jubilee Mendeleev Congress on General and Applied Chemistry (St. Petersburg, September).

For information:

UNESCO

Isabelle Brugnon, Web Editor, Natural Sciences Sector

7 Place de Fontenoy
75007 Paris, France
Phone: (33) 1 45 68 05 43
E-mail: i.brugnon@unesco.org
Web: www.iypt2019.org
Twitter: #IYPT2019

INTERNATIONAL UNION OF PURE AND APPLIED CHEMISTRY

Dr. Lynn M. Soby, Executive Director

PO Box 13757
Research Triangle Park, NC 27709
Phone: (919) 485 8700
E-mail: lsoby@iupac.org
Web: www.iupac.org
Twitter: @IUPAC and #iupac100

International Year of Indigenous Language

Jan 1–Dec 31, 2019

As part of a 2017 resolution on the rights of the world's indigenous peoples, the UN General Assembly proclaimed 2019 as the International Year of Indigenous Languages, a yearlong series of action-oriented activities focusing on "the critical risks confronting indigenous languages and the significance of such risks for sustainable development, reconciliation, good governance and peace-building." Language in general plays a crucial role in people's identity, social integration and development, while indigenous languages in particular impact a wider range of indigenous issues, including education, scientific and technological development, biosphere and the environment, freedom of expression, employment and social inclusion. Per UNESCO, 90 percent of the world's languages could disappear before 2099.

With UNESCO serving as the lead agency, the International Year unites educators, governments, activists, cultural organizations, athletes and goodwill ambassadors to coordinate events, curricula and initiatives to celebrate the more than 7,000 languages still spoken. The International Year website showcases communication campaigns, documentary shorts and a calendar of events including exhibitions, concerts, film festivals and sports and games festivals, including a launch event at the UNESCO headquarters in Paris and the biannual World Indigenous Nations Games (still in planning at press time).

For information:

UNESCO

Irmgarda Kasinskaite-Buddeberg, Programme Specialist

7 Place de Fontenoy
75352 Paris, France

Phone: (33) 1 45 68 16 45
E-mail: i.kasinskaite@unesco.org
Web: https://en.unesco.org/IY2019

Abdication of Emperor Akihito

Apr 30, 2019

On Apr 30, Japan's 85-year-old Emperor Akihito, citing failing health, abdicates, becoming the first Japanese monarch in 200 years to step down from the Chrysanthemum Throne. He is succeeded on May 1 by his son, Crown Prince Naruhito.

Akihito was born Dec 23, 1933, succeeding his father, wartime Emperor Hirohito, on the throne upon his death in 1989. Under Japanese law, an emperor may not descend, so parliament passed a historic one-time bill to allow Akihito to retire, with the stipulation that the Emperor's Birthday national holiday be moved from December 23 to February 23 (Naruhito's birthday). Culture Day on November 3 is the birthday of Emperor Meiji (reigned 1867–1912), and Showa Day on Apr 29 celebrates the late Hirohito's birthday; because Akihito is still living, his existing Dec 23 national holiday will be moved or renamed in order to prevent suggestions of dual authority.

Apr 30 was carefully chosen as the abdication date to follow Akihito's 30th anniversary jubilee on Feb 12 and coincide with the annual Golden Week national holiday period. The government is considering making both Apr 30 and May 1 national holidays, turning the Golden Week holiday into a consecutive 10-day holiday going forward. Akihito's abdication will mark the end of the Heisei era.

For information:

FOREIGN PRESS CENTER JAPAN

Media Relations Division

6F Nippon Press Center Building
2-2-1
Uchisaiwaicho, Chiyoda-ku
Tokyo 100-0011 Japan
Phone: (81) 3-3501-3405/5070
E-mail: ma@fpcjpn.or.jp
Web: http://fpcj.jp/en/

Total Solar Eclipse

July 2, 2019

A relatively long total eclipse of the sun takes place in the late afternoon of July 2 when the new moon passes directly in front of the sun in the southern hemisphere. The event will plunge a 124-mile-wide swatch into total darkness for 4 minutes and 32 seconds at the eclipse's greatest magnitude. The low-horizon eclipse will begin in the southern Pacific Ocean near the Pitcairn Islands and arc over the South Pacific, across a narrow slice of Chile to Argentina, where it will conclude at 5:46 PM local time over the far western suburbs of Buenos Aires. Sunset will occur about 10 minutes later. The partial solar eclipse will also be visible in Ecuador, Brazil, Uruguay and Paraguay, weather permitting (July is winter in the southern hemisphere).

The world's last total solar eclipse cut across the United States on Aug 21, 2017, lasting 2 minutes and 40 seconds. Astronomers without Borders, a California-based nonprofit organization that uses astronomy to unite people around the world, diverted from landfills thousands of 2017 eclipse-viewing glasses and recycled them for redistribution to schools in Argentina and Chile for the 2019 solar eclipse. A second total solar eclipse will cross Chile and Argentina 531 days later on Dec 14, 2020.

Transit of Mercury

Nov 11, 2019

A transit of Mercury is when the planet nearest the sun passes directly between Earth and the face of the sun. (The orbits of Mercury and Venus lie inside that of Earth, so they are the only planets that can pass between Earth and the sun to produce a transit.) During the next transit on Nov 11, 2019, Mercury will have an angular diameter (or apparent size) of 10 arc-seconds compared to an apparent size of 1,902 arc-seconds for the sun, appearing as a black speck just 1/158th the sun's size. Because this transit lasts 5 hours and 30 minutes, from 12:35 to 18:04 UTC, at least part of the event will be visible over most of the globe as Earth rotates. The transit will be visible in South America, Antarctica, eastern North America, southern tip of Greenland, a small slice of western Africa and the Atlantic Ocean.

Transits of Mercury may occur in either May or November; during the November transits, like this one, Mercury appears smaller than in May transits (10 arc-seconds versus 12 arc-seconds). May transits are rarer; the last May one occurred in 2016, and the next won't occur until May 7, 2049. The last November transit occurred in 2006 and will occur again in 2032 and 2039.

For those viewing this rare event, a properly filtered telescope is necessary, as the planet is too small to be visible to the naked eye and any viewing of the sun is dangerous.

Major 2019 Quadrennial and Biennial Sporting Events

Special Olympics World Summer Games
Mar 14–21

The first International Special Olympics Competition was held July 20, 1968, at Soldier Field, Chicago, IL. Since then, this inclusive movement, founded in 1968 by Eunice Kennedy Shriver, has grown to be one of the largest sporting and humanitarian events on the planet. Alternating between summer and winter games, this is the flagship event of the Special Olympics movement, which promotes equality, tolerance and acceptance around the world. Abu Dhabi, United Arab Emirates, is the host city for the 2019 summer games, which expect 500,000 spectators watching 7,000 athletes from 170 countries compete. There are 20,000 volunteers in addition to upward of 8,000 family members, coaches and friends.

For information:

Special Olympics World Games/Abu Dhabi 2019

Web: www.specialolympics.org

ICC Cricket World Cup
May 30–July 14

Ten cities (and 11 venues) in England and Wales cohost the 12th International Cricket Council (ICC) Cricket World Cup in 2019, where 10 teams participate in a round-robin-style tournament. Australia is the defending 2015 champion, and it is also the winningest nation, with five victories. First held in 1975 in England, the Cricket World Cup boasts a TV/online viewership of at least 1 billion people—about 20 percent of the world's population will be waiting for the results of 45 matches, knockout matches and the final at Lord's Cricket Ground, St. John's Wood, London.

For information:

ICC Cricket World Cup

Web: www.icc-cricket.com

FIFA Women's World Cup
June 7–July 7

The world's largest women's sporting event, held every four years, takes place in France in 2019. Since the Women's World Cup was first held in 1991 (when the US women's soccer team triumphed), it has grown dramatically in attendance and audience. In 2011, when the tournament was held in Germany, Japan became the first Asian team to hoist the World Cup in a win emotionally dedicated to those who had suffered in the Mar 11 earthquake and tsunami. The United States is the defending 2015 champion. In 2015, the tournament was expanded to 24 teams (from 16). In France 2019, these cities are hosts: Paris, Lyon, Nice, Valenciennes, Reims, Le Havre, Grenoble, Rennes and Montpellier. The opening match will be contested at the Parc des Princes, in Paris, and the cup final will be played at Lyon's Parc Olympic Lyonnais.

For information:

Fédération Internationale de Football Association (FIFA)

Web: www.fifa.com/womensworldcup/index.html

Copa America
June 14–July 7

Multinational soccer tournament ("American Cup") to be held in Brazil. Twelve teams battle it out: 10 from the CONMEBOL federation of South America and two guests from the Asian Football Confederation: Qatar and Japan. Chile is the defending champion.

For information:

CONMEBOL

Web: www.conmebol.com

Pan American Games/Parapan Am Games
July 26–Aug 11; Aug 23–Sept 1

First held in 1951, the Pan American Games are one of the largest multisport competitions in the world. Its 7,000 athletes come from throughout the Americas—drawn from the 41 nations of the Pan American Sports Organization (PASO), based in Mexico. The 2019 games will be held in Lima, Peru, and feature 423 events in 39 sports. The Parapan American Games were first held in 1999, and in 2019 athletes will compete in 18 sports—an increase from previous competitions.

For information:

Lima2019 Pan Am/Parapan Am Games

Web: https://lima2019.pe

World Police and Fire Games: Chengdu 2019
Aug 8–18

One of the largest multisport, multivenue amateur athletic events in the world. These biennial games feature competitions in 56 events, ranging from weight-lifting to darts, and draw more than 12,000 competitors from police, fire and public safety agencies from more than 68 countries. The games encourage volunteerism and good citizenship, serve to educate young people on the benefits of sports and physical fitness and build new partnerships among public safety agencies, businesses and communities.

For information:

World Police and Fire Games

Web: chengdu2019wpfg.com or www.cpaf.org/5/.

The Walker Cup

Sept 7–8

A prestigious biennial golfing competition that pits amateur teams from the United States and Great Britain and Ireland against each other, the 2019 Walker Cup will be held at Royal Liverpool Golf Club in Hoylake, England. The 47th edition is a two-day event. The United States is the defending champion and leads the series, 36–9–1. The 2019 team captains are Craig Watson (GB&I) and Nathaniel Crosby (US, son of Bing Crosby).

For information:

USGA/Walker Cup

Web: https://walkercup.co.uk or www.royal-liverpool-golf.com/2019+Walker+Cup/

Rugby World Cup 2019

Sept 20–Nov 2

Governed by the International Rugby Board, the Rugby World Cup has grown into one of the world's top sporting events. It takes place every four years and was first held in 1987 by cohosts New Zealand and Australia. At first, 16 teams participated in the cup; now 20 teams make the final rounds—drawn from regional unions. The ninth Rugby World Cup will be hosted by Japan and held in 12 cities, with the semifinals and final in International Stadium, Yokohama.

For information:

International Rugby Board

Web: www.irb.com or www.rugbyworldcup.com